# END TIMES MATRIX
## (INCLUDING THE REVELATION)

## ROY STOUT

WESTBOW
PRESS®
A DIVISION OF THOMAS NELSON
& ZONDERVAN

WestBow Press books may be ordered through booksellers or by contacting:

WestBow Press
A Division of Thomas Nelson & Zondervan
1663 Liberty Drive
Bloomington, IN 47403
www.westbowpress.com
844-714-3454

All Scripture quotations are taken from the King James Version.

ISBN: 978-1-6642-6625-4 (sc)
ISBN: 978-1-6642-6626-1 (hc)
ISBN: 978-1-6642-6624-7 (e)

Library of Congress Control Number: 2022908617

Print information available on the last page.

WestBow Press rev. date:  08/16/2022

The author has tried to segregate and explain specific sections of scripture that will aid in your Christian walk of faith through life and prays that this work will glorify God and win others to Jesus.

Before beginning our study, we need to cover some basics. In order to understand the end times and Revelation it is best to know the prophets, especially, Daniel. Daniel and Revelation must be studied together. A basis for Revelation is Daniel's 70 weeks where each week consists of 7 years, not days. 7 X 70 = 490 years, Daniel and Ezekiel were cotemporaries. Both were captives in Babylon at the same time. Daniel served the government and the king. Ezekiel was the prophet to the captives.

Many have written about the end times and have documented their interpretation. No one knows for certain what will happen and when. For example, "when will Christ return?" Mk 13:32.

> 32 But of that day and that hour knoweth no man, no, not the angels which are in heaven, neither the Son, but the Father

The key verses are Daniel 10:25-27.

> **25** Know therefore and understand, *that* from the going forth of the commandment to **restore and to build Jerusalem unto the Messiah the Prince** *shall be* **seven weeks,** and **threescore and two weeks: the street shall be built again, and the wall,** even in troublous times.
>
> 26 And after threescore and two weeks shall Messiah be cut off, but not for himself: and the people of the prince that shall come shall destroy the city and the sanctuary; and the end thereof shall be with a flood, and unto the end of the war desolations are determined.

**27** And he shall confirm the covenant with many for one week: and in the midst of the week he shall cause the sacrifice and the oblation to cease, and for the overspreading of abominations he shall make *it* desolate, even until the consummation, and that determined shall be poured upon the desolate.

Verse 25 says it will take seven weeks (49 years) to rebuild Jerusalem after the return from captivity. This is item B on the End-Time Matrix shown below. Verse 26 takes us from Micah to the rapture of the believers (sixty two weeks or 434 years). We have gone through the inter-testament period, the resurrection of Jesus and rapture of the church. Our status is now sixty two weeks and 483 years done and one week and seven years to go.

| VERSE | WEEKS | YEARS |
|-------|-------|-------|
| 25 | 7 | 49 |
| | 62 | 434 |
| TOTAL | 69 | 483 |
| REMAINING | 1 | 7 |
| TOTAL | 70 | 490 |

The one remaining week (seven years) consists of two three and one half year periods; the Tribulation (three and one half years) then, the Great Tribulation (three and one half years). Following the Great Tribulation is the millennium, the return of Christ to set up His kingdom on earth, the bounding of satan for 1,000 years, distribution of the land, establishment of the Jews on earth and creation of the new Jerusalem separate from earth.

Satan made a deal to honor the seven year period with Israel as a good little boy but, broke his promise half way through (three and one half years). He became violent during the last 3 1/2 years (Great Tribulation). God had no restrictions on satan during this time.

How to use the following matrix. The first entry is the Babylon Captivity and is designated as item A. Following the entire matrix are all of the chart's items beginning with "A." Go to item A and It will give you all the information about the captivity. Some of the items such as item C has a numeral "one1." Numerals are appendices.

| Babylon captivity | Cyrus the Great, King of Persia decrees that the temple be rebuilt. 538 BC The temple, walls and the city were restored. 49 years, 1week | The silent years from Micah to the crucifixion. 434 years 62 weeks  Total thus far 483 years 69 weeks  Remaining 1 week 7 years  (1) | The church age and the Revelation. | Rapture of the church | The apostasy false non-raptured Church  Called The Harlot in chapter 17. |
|---|---|---|---|---|---|
| A | B | C | D | E | F |

| The 7 churches of Turkey. Let's talk turkey | The Tribulation  3 ½ year ½ week | Temple is built. | Abomination of deso-lation. | The great tribulation. Daniel's 70 weeks are fulfilled. | 7 Seals | 144,000 Sealed. |
|---|---|---|---|---|---|---|
| G | H | I | J | K | L | M |

| 7 Trumpets | 2 witnesses | 7 personages | 7 vials | Armageddon (4,5) | Lamb is married (7) | Babylon falls |
|---|---|---|---|---|---|---|
| N | O | P | Q | R | S | T |

| Millennium | Christ returns to set up His kingdom. Satan is bound for 1000 years. | The first resurrection. | Land is assigned, those sealed, gates named. | God brings the dead sea to life. | Jesus splits a mountain. Israel gets a seaport. | Satan is loosen. Gog/Magaog war. |
|---|---|---|---|---|---|---|
|  |  | (10) | (3) | (6) | (8) | (2,5) |
| U | U1 | U2 | U3 | U4 | U5 | V |
| All "U" designations occur during the millennium. | | | | | | |

| Satan is thrown into the Lake of fire. | The Bema judgment seat of Christ. Great White Throne Judgment | Second Resurrection (10) | Death and hell casted into the Lake of Fire. | A new heaven and earth. No sea. | God dwells with Christians. |
|---|---|---|---|---|---|
| W | X | Y | Z | AA | AB |

| New Jerusalem | Water of Life. Tree of Life | Promise of Christ's return. (9) | Final call for salvation. Eternity begins |
|---|---|---|---|
| AC | AD | AE | AF |

## A – Babylonian Captivity

It lasted 70 years. Why? Ex 23:10-11.

> EX23:10 And six years thou shalt sow thy land, and
> shalt gather in the fruits thereof:

EX 23:11 **But the seventh year thou shalt let it rest** and lie still;
that the poor of thy people may eat: and what they leave the beasts of
the field shall eat. In like manner thou shalt deal with thy vineyard,
and with thy olive yard. EX 25:1-4,20

> EX 25:1 And the LORD spake unto Moses in mount
> Sinai, saying,

> EX 25:2 Speak unto the children of Israel, and say
> unto them, When ye come into the land which I
> give you, then shall the land **keep a sabbath unto
> the LORD.**

> EX 25:3 Six years thou shalt sow thy field, and six
> years thou shalt prune thy vineyard, and gather in
> the fruit thereof;

> EX 25:4 But **in the seventh year shall be a sabbath
> of rest unto the land, a sabbath for the LORD:
> thou shalt neither sow thy field, nor prune thy
> vineyard.** (Lev. 25:1–7)

The seventh-year sabbath was called *shimita*.

> EX25:20 And if ye shall say, **What shall we eat the
> seventh year?** behold, we shall not sow, nor gather
> in our increase:

25:21 Then **I will command my blessing upon you in the sixth year, and it shall bring forth fruit for three years.** (Lev. 25:20–21)

The Jews had not kept the shimita sabbath for 490 years. Why? It was a good deal. Work one year (sixth year) and get paid for three (490/7=70 years). This was the length of the captivity. This proves that God is concerned about the land. Christians should consider themselves landlords of the Lord's land. I have traveled in all fifty USA states except two and have witnessed the trash that has been thrown from cars. This is an insult to God. We must consider ourselves landlords of the Lord's land.

### B – Cyrus, King of Persia, Decrees the Temple to Be Rebuilt

Thank God for Cyrus. Today, Persia is Iran. Iran and Israel are far from being friends. Iran calls Israel a stinking corpse that should be removed. The temple walls and the city were restored. Zerubbabel built the temple. Ezra restored the law of Moses. Nehemiah rebuilt the city and walls. This took forty-nine years (one week). It is the first of Daniel's seventy weeks.

### C – The Silent Years from Micah to the Crucifixion (434 years/seven = 62 weeks). Time expended thus far is the following:

| Item | Years | Weeks | Activity |
|------|-------|-------|----------|
| B | 49 | 7 | Rebuild Jerusalem |
| C | 434 | 62 | From Micah to Jesus |
| Total | 483 | 69 | One week left; it is the tribulation |

There is one week remaining, and that is the tribulation (three and a half years) and the great tribulation (three and a half years) for a total of seven years or one week. This is Daniel's last (seventieth) week. It will begin after the true church is raptured.

Ruling nations over Israel between the testaments were *(Halley's Bible Handbook;* 22nd edition, Zondervan Publishing House) the following:[1]

- Persia 536 BC–333 BC (203 years)
- Greece 333 BC–323 BC (10 years)
- Egypt 321 BC–204 BC (119 years)
- Syria 204 BC–165 BC (39 years)
- Maccabean 165 BC–63 BC (102 years; a period of Jewish independence)
- Rome 63 BC–AD 313 (376 years; Christ lived in an occupied country; see appendix 1.

## D – The Church Age

This began with the ascension of Jesus and will end with His return to begin the millennium and establish His kingdom on earth. It is ongoing today. There is one week (seven years) of Daniel's seventy weeks left.

The Revelation: John sees Jesus (Rev. 1:9–16). Jesus tells John to write to the seven churches that are in Asia Minor (Turkey). See item G. Let's talk Turkey!

Jesus is sitting between candlesticks. He is holding stars (Rev. 1:19). John is told to write about things that are now (the present) and things that will be hereafter (the future) (Rev. 1:20). The stars are the angels of the seven churches and the candlesticks are the seven churches.

---
[1]

## E – Rapture of the True Church

The church consists of those who are truly saved. In 2000 a Canadian American film appeared titled *Left Behind*. The subject was the rapture. People were disappearing (the saved) while others were not (unsaved). Many were amazed that they were not raptured. The only ones raptured were those who trusted Jesus as their Savior and lived a Christian life that proved it. The church in heaven is now the priesthood of believers. God's throne was surrounded by a sea of glass representing the holiness of God. The four living creatures were the following:

- lion – the king; represents the Gospel of Matthew; Jesus is the king
- calf (ox) – beast of burden; represents Mark, the servant
- man – Luke talked about the son of man
- eagle – Gospel of John

The twenty-four elders represent the twelve tribes of Israel plus the twelve apostles.

Those raptured will live in the New Jerusalem. Only Christians will be raptured. What is a Christian? One who has put one's faith in Jesus as Savior and has not relied on anything one has done. Faith is

Forsake
All;
I
Trust
Him.

Faith, followed by baptism, is a proper start. Now your life must reflect the new life you have in Jesus. Faith changes from a noun to a verb and becomes something Christians do. James 2:14, 17-20.

14 What *doth it* profit, my brethren, though a man say he hath faith, and have not works? can faith save him.

17 **Even so faith, if it hath not works, is dead, being alone.**

18 Yea, a man may say, Thou hast faith, and I have works: shew me thy faith without thy works, and I will shew thee my faith by my works.

19 Thou believest that there is one God; thou doest well: the devils also believe, and tremble.

20 But wilt thou know, O vain man, that **faith without works is dead?**

We need to pay attention to who is talking. James was the eldest of Jesus' four brothers. When Jesus was crucified, James was about thirty-one. He had spent most of that time growing up with Jesus. Although the brothers of Jesus did not believe in Him at first, they eventually did so. Jude wrote the epistle of Jude, and James wrote James. He then became the leader of the Christian church in Jerusalem. The bottom line is James spent decades listening to Jesus; he heard Jesus speak more than anybody.

What is James really saying that seems to contradict the statement "Once saved, always saved"? He is saying that if you are a true Christian, your life will show it. Christianity is not a club you join and don't attend. Ask yourself,

> "If I were on trial for being a Christian, would there be enough evidence to convict me?"

If you took an oath to become a soldier but refused to salute the flag, wear the uniform, or take orders, are you a soldier? Some would say yes because you took an oath. Really? If you are in the navy, your next home is the brig. The other branches of the military use the Leavenworth DB (Discipline Barracks) at Fort Leavenworth, Kansas. God refuses to accept inactivity. Luke 6:46 says,

> "And why call ye me, Lord, Lord, and do not the things which I say?"

He will not accept do-nothing Christians. Matthew 7:20-23.

> 20 Wherefore **by their fruits ye shall know them.**
>
> 21 **Not every one** that saith unto me, Lord, Lord, shall enter into the kingdom of heaven; but he that doeth the will of my Father which is in heaven.
>
> 22 Many will say to me in that day, Lord, Lord, have we not prophesied in thy name? and in thy name have cast out devils? and in thy name done many wonderful works?
>
> 23 **And then will I profess unto them, I never knew you: depart from me, ye that work iniquity.**
> (Matt. 7:20–23; emphasis mine)

The statement "Once saved, always saved" should read, "Once *truly* saved, always saved." The works you do after you are truly saved earn you rewards.

## F – Apostasy of the Non-Raptured False Church (Rev. 17:1–2)

Those who remained (the lost) formed the apostasy church. Apostasy is renunciation of a religious faith. One may argue people can be non-Christians because they have never heard the gospel preached, but many have! Some left behind will be church members. Some will be the cults and isms, of which the USA has thousands. Some will be excited to see the church leave. Now they can live as they please and not have to answer to God. This starts the tribulation period. It is Daniel's seventieth (last) week of seven years. The seven years occur in two three-and-a-half-year periods: the tribulation and the great tribulation.

*The harlot* rides the wild beast. Revelation 17:1–5 says the harlot is the false (apostate) church and the wild beast is the restored Rome. The beast and false prophet will destroy the harlot church once it has served their purpose. The beast is antichrist. Could this be referring to the Catholic Church or some other organization? Scarlet is the color of the Roman Catholics, and red is the color of Roman imperialism.

### Revelation 17:8–10

The seven heads are seven mountains where the woman lives. Rome has seven hills. There are seven kings; five are gone, one is living now, and one is yet to come. Past kings are Caesar, Tiberius, Caligula, Claudius, and Nero. The present king is Domitian, who ruled during John's life. The future king is the antichrist. He is the little horn of Daniel 7.

**G – The seven churches of Turkey.** Let's talk Turkey. Revelation chapters 1 – 4 addresses the seven churches of Asia Minor (now Turkey). There were churches other than these seven. Why didn't Christ include them? Scholars believe that the seven churches represent the character of all churches today. Two found favor with

God; Smyrna and Philadelphia. They are the only churches that exist today. Smyrna is now Izmir. Smyrna was the martyr church and Philadelphia was the missionary church. They both gave and operated outside the walls of the church.

**H – The Tribulation** 3 ½ years is the first the first 3 ½ period of Daniel's 70th week (7 years). It begins after the raptured church disappears in the clouds with Jesus. The Tribulation doesn't last very long. Dan 9:27.

> 27 And he shall confirm the covenant with many for one week and in the midst of the week he shall cause the sacrifice and the oblation to cease, and for the overspreading of abominations he shall make it desolate, even until the consummation and that determined shall be poured upon the desolate.

What is being said? Satan will go along with a seven year term but, in the middle of it, he will change his mind and attack anything that relates to God. This last 3 ½ years is referred to as the Great Tribulation and completes Daniel's 70 weeks.

**I – The Temple is rebuilt**. Ez 40-48. The three prophets that belong to this period are Haggai, Zechriah and Malachi. The temple they built would be modified by Herod then, destroyed by the Romans in 70AD. It is noteworthy that the time of the gentiles began with the captivity and will continue until Christ returns at the start of the millennium to set up His kingdom. This long period is when the Jews were ruled by the gentiles. Thus far, it has been about 2500 years.

The first temple was built by Solomon. He hired David's friend Hiram, King of Phoenicia to build it. The next temple was built by Zerubbabel after the Babylonian captivity. About 20BC King Herod finished upgrading the temple. In 70AD the Romans destroyed it. Emperor Julian (361-363 tried to rebuild the temple but failed. Today, the Muslim Dome of the Rock sits atop the temple base. The next temple will be built during the millennium as discussed in Ezekiel 40-48.

## J – The abomination of desolation.

This is discussed in Daniel 9:27 (see above). Oblation is a religious sacrifice. Desolation means extreme discuss. Desolation means the people will flee when they see the abomination. Jesus spoke about this in Mark 13:14-20.

> 14 But when ye shall see the abomination of desolation, spoken of by Daniel the prophet, standing where it ought not, (let him that readeth understand,) then let them that be in Judaea flee to the mountains:
>
> 15 And let him that is on the housetop not go down into the house, neither enter therein, to take anything out of his house:
>
> 16 And let him that is in the field not turn back again for to take up his garment.
>
> 17 But woe to them that are with child, and to them that give suck in those days!
>
> 18 And pray ye that your flight be not in the winter.
>
> 19 For in those days shall be affliction, such as was not from the beginning of the creation which God created unto this time, neither shall be.

> 20 And except that the Lord had shortened those
> days, no flesh should be saved: but for the elect's
> sake, whom he hath chosen, he hath shortened the
> days.

God is telling them to flee. Why is this happening? Remember that God has unleased satan to do whatever he wants to do. The abomination of desolation is a slap in the face to God and He is slapping back. This is the worst time man has ever had or will ever have again.

We will read later that God creates a hail storm with hail stones weighing 100 pounds. A concrete block weighs about 28 pounds. Tie 4 of them together and drop them on your head. This is equivalent to God's hailstone. During events like these, plus others such as wars, many women and children are killed.

**K – The Great Tribulation.** The Great Tribulation lasts 3 ½ years. Daniel 12:11.

> 11 And from the time that the daily sacrifice shall
> be taken away, and the abomination that maketh
> desolate set up, there shall be a thousand two
> hundred and ninety days.

When it ends, Christ returns to set up His earthly kingdom with the Jews, binds satan for 1,000 years and begins the millennium.

Antichrist stops the temple sacrifices and places a disgusting idol in it for 1260 days which is 3 ½ years (1/2 week). This begins the Great Tribulation and is the last half of Daniel's 70th week. The Great Tribulation is the greatest horror the world has ever known. It has been referred to as "the time of Jacob's trouble."

The abomination is going to make the cities desolate. It is also going to make God angry and He will direct His wrath on the Jews for their rejection of Him. It boggles the mind how someone can hear god talking to them yet, not obey what He says. If God talked to you today, would that get your attention? Most of us would probably faint. The Jews not only ignored Him, they disobeyed Him. They remind me of a spoiled child with loving parents.

### L – The 7 seals

**First seal.** The white horse is released to conquer.

**Second Seal**. The red horse is released to remove peace from the earth,

**Third seal.** The black horse was released to bring famine on the land. Famine usually followed a war.

**Fourth seal.** A pale colored horse was released. Death and Hades were the riders. They had the authority to kill ¼ of the earth's population. That is nearly 2 billion people. See appendix 11.

**Fifth Seal** – John saw the souls of millions of believers that were martyred. They wanted vengeance but were told to wait because more would join them.

**Sixth seal** – Environmental events. Eartquakes, sun turned black, moon became as blood, stars fell, mountains and islands moved.

**M – 144,000 sealed**. God selected 144,000 (12,000 from each tribe) and seal them with protection against any harm. The were Jewish evangelists. The Holy Spirit is the seal for a Christian.

## N – The seven trumpets.

The **first trumpet**. 1/3 of the earth, the trees and grass were burned up.

The **second trumpet** caused the seas to turn to blood causing 1/3 of sea life to die and 1/3 of all ships to be destroyed.

The **third trumpet** caused a star named wormwood to fall to earth and polluted the water causing many to die.

The **fourth trumpet** caused 1/3 of the sun, moon and stars to lose their light.

The **fifth trumpet** sounds and John saw a star falling from heaven and having the key to the bottomless pit. The star was Lucifer (satan). The bottomless pit is an abuyss which is a "holding cell" for demons already found guilty and await the Great White Throne Judgment of God.

John saw locust come out of the pit. They were allowed to torment people for 5 months but, not to kill them. They had a king named Abaddon in the Hebrew and Apollygon in the Greek.

The **sixth trumpet** released four demonic angels from the Euphrates River. They have permission to kill 1/3 of the unbelievers. See appendix 11. John heard the size of the army to be 200,000,000. This would lead one to think of an eastern country such as China. They could muster twice that amount.

NOTE! We notice the fraction that appear above such as 1/3. Why? It is God's wish that people repent but, matters got worst. When we get to the bowls (vials) we see that the fractions go away and the whole earth is involved.

**O – The two witnesses.** God gives them authority to prophesy for 3 ½ years. Their identity is not given. Most people think they are Elijah and Elisha? They are killed then resurrected to ascend. See appendix 11.

**P – The five personages.**

1 – **The woman** gives birth. The child is Jesus and the woman is Israel.

2 – **The Dragon.** It is satan. He has seven heads and ten horns. The seven heads are seven empires and the ten horns are the form of government the antichrist will rule.

3 – **Michael** wages war with satan in heaven and wins. God throws satan out of heaven.

4 – **Antichrist** is the beast out of the sea. The word antichrist is not in Revelation, it only appears in John's epistles. People will want him to rule. He will be clever, convincing and attractive. He will be a gentile. He will be followed and worshipped.

5 – **The False prophet**, the beast out of the earth. He will assist the antichrist. He will institute the "666" mark of the beast.

**Q – The 7 bowls (vials).** Unlike previous judgments that involved a portion of the earth such as 1/3, these cover all of the earth. These judgments are for unbelievers.

The **first bowl** gave the people who had the mark of the beast (666) malignant skin boils.

The **second bowl** killed all of the sea life and turned the seas into blood.

The **third bowl** contaminated all fresh water sources by turning them into blood.

The **fourth bowl** caused the sun to emit scorching rays of heat.

The **fifth bowl** cause the sun to bring darkness.

The **sixth bowl** cause the Euphrates river to dry up to allow passage for the kings of the east. John saw the evil trinity (dragon, antichrist and false prophet) that had demons like frogs coming out of their mouths. They will gather the nations that are against Israel unto Megiddo. See appendix 4.

### R – Armageddon (Rev. 16:13–21; Rev. 19:17–18)

There are varying opinions about Armageddon and the Gog/Magog wars. Some say they are the same war. There are too many differences to say they are the same war. Of significance is where they are mentioned in scripture. Armageddon is chapter 16, and Gog/Magog is chapter 20. If they were the same war, why does John separate them by one thousand years (the millennium) here? See appendices 4 and 5.

**S – Lamb Is Married.** Where will the church be during the seventieth week of Daniel 9—the last seven years prior to the Second Coming of Christ, which has been popularly called the tribulation period? The church will be in heaven with Christ during that period. The church is the Lamb's bride. The marriage is in heaven and the supper on earth. See Appendix 7.

The church will be in the New Jerusalem, a 1500 mile cube that is separate from earth. The Jews will occupy the earth and the Christians will occupy the New Jerusalem.

**T –Babylon falls. Rev 18.** Babylon has always been a source of evil beginning with Nimrod who tried to build the tower of Babel to reach heaven. This is thought to be the Babylon that was restored by the antichrist. Verse 8 says its demise was quick. Verse 10 says it was even quicker. Rev 18:8-10.

> 8 Therefore shall her plagues come in one day, death, and mourning, and famine; and she shall be utterly burned with fire: for strong is the Lord God who judgeth her.

> 9 And the kings of the earth, who have committed fornication and lived deliciously with her, shall bewail her, and lament for her, when they shall see the smoke of her burning,

> 10 Standing afar off for the fear of her torment, saying, Alas, alas, that great city Babylon, that mighty city! for **in one hour is thy judgment come.**

We are talking about a lavish city being burned in one hour. We don't know the size of the city but, one hour indicates a nuclear strike or God intervened and set fire to it?

**U – The Millennium.** This is 1,000 years of peace where satin is bound. The Great Tribulation has just ended, as did Daniel's 70th week, and Christ has returned to establish His kingdom. This is Christ's third trip to earth. Two were touchdowns and one was a fly by. The first touch-down (landing) was His birth. The second one is His return after the Great Tribulation. The fly-by was the rapture.

**U1 – Christ returns to set up His kingdom on earth.** First things first; satan is bound for 1,000 years (a millennium). There are many verses describing Jesus earthly kingdom during the 1000 years of peace. All nations will worship Him. The church will travel to earth to help him rule and earth will travel to the New Jerusalem to worship. Jesus will have His saved ones in the New Jerusalem and the Jews on earth. Although there does appear to be travel, the Jews will dominate earth and the Christians the New Jerusalem.

**U2 – The 1st Ressurection.** See appendix 10.

**U3 – The land is assigned to the 12 tribes, the 144,000 sealed Jews, and gate assignments are made to each tribe.** See Appendix 3.

This is happening during the millennium when there is peace. God told the Israelis to take 330,000 square miles of land in Canaan and they took 30,000 square miles. This is less than 10%. Ezekiel does not tell us how many square miles was given to them.

**U4 – The Dead Sea is made alive.** See appendix 6.

**U5 – Israel gets a seaport, Jesus splits a mountain and the Dead Sea is healed.** See Appendix 8.

**V – Satan is let loose. Gog/Magog war.** EZ 38-39 talks about Gog/Magog when Satan is loosed after the 1.000 years millennium. It is satans' last chance for supremacy. Rev 20:7-8.

> **7** And when the thousand years are expired, Satan shall be loosed out of his prison,
>
> **8** And shall go out to deceive the nations which are in the four quarters of the earth, Gog and Magog, to gather them together to battle: the number of whom is as the sand of the sea.

See Appendices 2.

**W - Satan thrown into the lake of fire and brim stone.** The beast and the false prophet that instigated Armageddon were already cast into the Lake of Fire prior to satan1,000 years ago Rev 20:10. God gave satan one more shot at conversion when he initiated the Gog/Magog war.

**X - The Great White Throne Judgment and the Bema (Judgment) seat of Christ.** Rev 20:1-13. This is the end of the line. Some may call it a formality. If your name is not in the book, you are lost. Then why have a judgment? Verse 13 says "they were judged every man according to his works." Works can't save you but, this verse tends to reflect on the degree of punishment you get. It is a fact that some of the unsaved do more good deeds and act more like Christians than do Christians. We may think about degrees of punishment as we do degrees of rewards such as the crowns or the Bema seat. It is similar to knowing someone that has superior skills in something (i.e., sports, acting, etc.) but, refuses to sign a contract (accept Jesus as their savior).

**The Bema (Judgment) Seat of Christ.** Scholars believe this will occur just prior to the Great White Throne Judgment and involve five crowns i.e., (Contribution; Wikipedia; Crowns in heaven – reward for the faithful.)

1 – Imperishable Crown – 1 Cor 9:24-25
2 – Crown of Rejoicing – I Thess 2:19
3 – Crown of Righteousness 2 Tim 4:18
4 – Crown of Glory – I Pet 5:4
5 – Crown of Life – Rev 2:10

It is also a place where rewards will be given or lost depending how one has used his/her life for the Lord.

**Y – The 2nd resurrection.** See Appendix 10.

**Z - Death and hell were cast into the lake of fire.** Rev 20:14-15.

This means total separation from God. Heaven is where God is and hell is where he isn't. I imagine God gave a sigh of relief having gone all the way from Genesis to this point. Part of this occurred in Eph 4:8-10. In the Old Testament when Jews died they went to Sheol. It consisted of the following compartments;

Abraham's Bosum or paradise ... ... the great gulf ... ... Gehenna
or Hades

When Christ died He descended to sheol (see Luke 16:19-31) and led captivity captive i.e., he led the saved from paradise to heaven. In the Old Testament, it was called sheol. The Greeks called it Hades. The English call it hell. Hades is now the "holding cell" for the lost who have died. They will be resurrected for the Great White Throne judgment and sent to hell.

**AA new heaven and a new earth, no sea. Rev 21:1-3.**

> 1 And I saw a new heaven and a new earth: for the first heaven and the first earth were passed away; and **there was no more sea.**
> 2 And I John saw the holy city, **new Jerusalem,** coming down from God out of heaven, prepared as a bride adorned for her husband.
> 3 And I heard a great voice out of heaven saying, Behold, the tabernacle of God is with men, and he will dwell with them, and they shall be his people, and **God himself shall be with them,** and be their God.

Some of us upgrade our homes as they age due to wear. Talk about an upgrade! God is replacing the earth and heaven. Wow! Be aware that the bible is talking about a new earth, heaven and Jerusalem.

1 – new earth – an update of what we have now.

2 – new heaven – Heaven was not all good and no bad. Satan rebelled against God as did many angels and were ejected from heaven. Michael and satan fought a war in heaven. Perhaps God thought it best to sanctify heaven by renewing it. He didn't upgrade it, He replaced it. Now heaven is pure again.

Notice that there is no more sea on earth. That means there is no more water cycle i.e., rain, rivers or run-off. This use to mean a famine but, God has eliminated famines. Famines were mentioned 13 times in scripture and they all were punishments inflicted on Israel. It won't happen again. No more sea means no ice caps, ice bergs, sea life, or ships. If God allows it (remember, He is living with us) we can walk from New York City USA to London England. The ocean bottom has mountain ranges like those we can now see on land. We have an eternity to explore the entire globe. Wildlife will not be a problem. Isaiah 11:6.

> 6 The wolf also shall dwell with the lamb, and the leopard shall lie down with the kid; and the calf and the young lion and the fatling together; and a little child shall lead them.

This is especially appealing to me because I ran a trap line as a teenager and enjoyed camping in the mountains. I have seen a bear and bobcat and avoided them. What a difference it will be to not fear them.

**AB - God dwells with Christians**. Rev 21:22-23. There was no temple. There is no temple in the New Jerusalem but there is on earth with the Jews. There was no sun or moon because God and Jesus were the light. We are use to thinking of heaven as the only place for the resurrected. THE CHRISTIANS WILL BE IN THE NEW JERUSALEM AND THE JEWS IN THE NEW EARTH. There will be plenty of traffic between the two because they will have to travel to the New Jerusalem to worship as Christians. Rev 21:24. This is a new concept for Christians and Jews. The Christians were promised heaven and they got it as the New Jerusalem. The Jews were promised Canaan and they got it as the New Earth.

## AC – The new Jerusalem

Notice in verse Rev 21:2 that John saw the New Jerusalem (1500 mile cube) coming down from heaven but, it never landed. Why? It would cover all of Israel. If you placed it in the USA, it would cover 90% of it and some of Mexico. It was meant to be detached from earth.

Matt 24:29 tells us the moon and sun will not provide light after the tribulation. Not a problem! Rev 22:23 says God and Jesus are the source of the light. It must rotate or half of the earth would always be dark.

How will the New Jerusalem house all of the saved Christians? Remember, it is a 1500 mile cube. 1500 X 1500 X 1500 = 34,875,000,000 Cubic Miles. The current world population is about **7,700,000,000. Revelation 9:15-16 tells us that 200,000,000 horsemen were to "slay the third part of men." 7,700,000,000 X 1/3 = 2,6 00,000,000. This leaves 4,400,000,000 men. Actually, the real number would be less because of the calamities that occurred prior to this action. Is we divide the cubic miles by the**

**amount of men we get eight cubic miles per person.** Here is what Jesus said. John 14:2.

> 2 In my Father's house are many mansions: if it were not so, I would have told you. I go to prepare a place for you.

This is the new Jerusalem, the bride of Christ and home of the Christians.

We may also have the ethereal ability to pass through doors as did Jesus. At one point after His resurrection He told them not to touch Him because He had not ascended to the father. Later that same Day He said *touch me John 19:28*. It is obvious that He ascended to the Father between those statements. Perhaps we will have that interplanetary travel privilege? Could we explore the cosmos? Personally, I would rather not travel if I could stay with Jesus. What would be better than that?

Rev 21:17 -20 tells us the city is made of gold. The foundations are also made of gems. Today, people that can afford it buy these gems and wear them on their fingers, ears, lips and noses. In the new Jerusalem, we will walk on them. It seems that God has pleased us by taking the gems from underground and processing them for our pleasure? I know my wife will be excited.

**AD - The Water of life and the tree of life.** Rev 22:1-2 The tree yielded fruit every month. No shortage of food. The leaves were for healing the nations. Rev 22:3-5. Verse 4 says "And they shall see His face." Finally!

**AE - Promise of His Return**. Rev 22:6- 16. He is coming back.

See Appendix 9 (When will Christ return?).

**AF - Final invitation, warning, promise and prayer.** Rev 22. Verses 18 and 19 warns against changing the prophecy that John wrote. Versus 20-21. Jesus promises to come "quickly" but, does not say when. We need to give some thought to when He will return. Why aren't we told? Think back to Micah, the last Old Testament prophet. He probably asked the same question. Prophet after prophet talked about Jesus as did the Psalms and other books. Where is He? They said He would come but, He didn't until the New Testament 400 years later. Why so long? Here are a few reasons.

1 – The players were not cast i.e., Judas. Pilate, Herod and more had not yet been born.

2 – Daniel's prophecy about the kings had not occurred. They were Babylon, Persia, Greece, Rome.

3 – Prophecies concerning the cross meant that Rome must have conquered Israel. The cross was their form of capital punishment.

4– If you were expecting company and knew when they were arriving, the house would be clean, the yard mowed and everyone well groomed. God wants to see us as we live.

5 – Probably the biggest reason for Jesus not returning to date is 2 Pet 3:9.

> 9 The Lord is not slack concerning his promise, as some men count slackness; **but is longsuffering to us-ward, not willing that any should perish, but that all should come to repentance.**

As I compare this life to heaven, I am amazed. No more checks. Everything is provided. Plenty of land for hiking. No fear of wildlife. No diseases. No hunger. No death. And best of all. God is with us. I want to spend the first 10,000 years just staring at Jesus. I do have some questions for Paul, David, Solomon, Moses and others. I am in my 80's and am amazed at the brethren of my age and their fear of dying. They should be excited. Think of being raptured and finding yourself looking at Jesus. What would I do? What would I say? How would I act other then praising God?

Final Comments.

What do we need to know about the end times? The book titled Revelation has been addressed by many authors trying to explain its contents. Some authors have criticized other author's interpretations. They have tried to sequence the events and identify the personages mentioned in the book. For example, the mark of the beast is stated as 666. There are different interpretations of what 666 means. In poker, tree sixes may be a winning hand but, not in Christianity. The apostle John did not tell us who it is, so we are left to guess. We would like to know the events of the end time that we may compare them to current events. When we see events such as floods, earthquakes, wars, moral degradation and etc. we tend to think that the end time is near. This has happened in all generations. The United States of America has been in over 100 wars (Congress approved engagements). The end did not come. During WWII millions of Jews were murdered during the holocaust in Germany. The end did not come. Some people have set dates and awaited the return of Jesus. The end did not come. Only God knows when the end will happen. Even Jesus does not know. Mark 13:32.

> **32** But of that day and *that* hour **knoweth no man,**
> no, not the angels which are in heaven, **neither the
> Son, but the Father.**

Suppose we need an operation to correct a life-threatening heart defect. The doctor examines us; blood tests, cardiogram, X-rays, MRI, etc. The doctor decides if we need the operation. We have the faith in him/her that he/she will make the right decision.

Notice that we had the operation without knowing all of the details. We could not interpret the X-rays, results of a blood test, read the cardiogram, or the results of the MRI. We did not know what chemical they injected to render us unconscious, the instruments they used in the operating room, or what they actually did during the operation. The sequence of events and the duration of them were all unknown. What we do know is that we went to sleep and, what seemed to be seconds later woke up in the recovery room. The events that occurred between the operating room and the recovery room are unknown.

This principle also applies to The Revelation. We just went through an operation without knowing all of the details. We can also go through The Revelation without knowing all of the details. It is good to study scripture and try to learn what it is saying to us. But it is not necessary to interpret every detail. We would be much better off growing and going as full time Christians to witness to win lost souls to Christ. It is nice but, not necessary to identify the people nor sequence the events in Revelation. Did Daniel know what he was writing? Dan 12:8.

> 8 And **I heard, but I understood not**: then said I,
> O my Lord, what *shall be* the end of these *things*?

The Holy Spirit was the author and Daniel the pen. 1 Peter 1:21.

> 21 For the prophecy came not in old time by the
> will of man: but holy men of God spake *as they were*
> moved by the Holy Ghost.

The world needs to hear the gospel. Of all the "signs" that exist, this is one where the Christian can make an impact on God's timeline for the return of Christ. Every Christian should sponsor all missionary efforts to translate then, preach the gospel in local languages worldwide. If all people had the written scripture in their own language one of the end time signs would be fulfilled. Could we accelerate God's timeline and hasten the return of Christ? Yes!

No one knows why the other apostles were not present. James, John and Peter were known as "the inner circle" of Jesus. Studying scripture is proper and will fuel you to grow and go. John 3:16 tells us to confess our sins and believe in Jesus and accept him as our savior. That's it! Knowing the end time events would be great but, to the Christian we know that we are on the winning side and will spend an eternity with God without knowing exactly what will happen and when. Christians are winners!

There is one more thing Christ told us relative to His second coming.

Mark 13:33.

> **33** Take ye heed, watch and pray: for ye know not when the time is.

It could happen NOW.

## APPENDICES

# APPENDIX 1

# BETWEEN THE TESTAMENTS

This is referred to as the Inter-Testament or 500 year Period and begins with the book of Micah. The countries that ruled Israel during this period are listed.

Contribution; Wikipedia, Sermon: What happened between the testaments.

| COUNTRY | DATES (BC) | YEARS |
|---|---|---|
| Persia | 536 – 333 | 203 |
| Greece | 333 – 323 | 10 |
| Egypt | 323 – 204 | 119 |
| Syria | 204 – 165 | 39 |
| Maccabean | 165 – 63 | 102 |
| Rome | 63 –4 (Christ) | 67 |
| TOTAL | | 540 |
| NOTE | Some reigns overlapped. | |
| NOTE | Rome ruled until 313AD | |

Beginning with Persia and ending with Rome is a staircase leading to Christ.

                                                    Christ
                                            Rome>>>>
                                    Maccabean>>>>
                            Syria>>>>
                    Egypt>>>>
            Greece>>>>
Persia>>>>

What was the status of the Jews at the beginning of this period? The Jews had been captured by Babylonia then Babylonia by Persia. Cyrus, the Persian emperor, issued a decree allowing the Jews to return to Israel. Zerubbel built the temple and Nehemiah rebuilt the walls, restored the rituals and became Governor. The Jewish state exited in Israel.

The fate of the world rulers during the 400 years was depicted in Daniel 2:31-45.

> **31** Thou, O king, sawest, and behold a great image. This great image, whose brightness *was* excellent, stood before thee; and the form thereof *was* terrible.

> **32** This image's **head *was* of fine gold**, his **breast and his arms of silver,** his **belly and his thighs of brass,**

> **33** His **legs of iron**, his **feet part of iron and part of clay.**

**34** Thou sawest till that **a stone** was cut out without hands, which smote the image upon his feet *that were* of iron and clay, and brake them to pieces.

**35** Then was **the iron, the clay, the brass, the silver, and the gold, broken to pieces together,** and became like the chaff of the summer threshing floors; and the wind carried them away, that no place was found for them: and **the stone that smote the image became a great mountain, and filled the whole earth.**

**36** This *is* the dream; and we will tell the interpretation thereof before the king.

**37 Thou, O king,** *art* **a king of kings**: for the God of heaven hath given thee a kingdom, power, and strength, and glory.

**38** And wheresoever the children of men dwell, the beasts of the field and the fowls of the heaven hath he given into thine hand, and hath made thee ruler over them all. **Thou** *art* **this head of gold.**

**39** And after thee **shall arise another kingdom** inferior to thee, and another **third kingdom of brass,** which shall bear rule over all the earth.

**40** And **the fourth kingdom shall be strong as iron**: forasmuch as iron breaketh in pieces and subdueth all *things*: and as iron that breaketh all these, shall it break in pieces and bruise.

**41** And whereas **thou sawest the feet and toes, part of potters' clay, and part of iron, the kingdom shall be divided;** but there shall be in it of the strength of the iron, forasmuch as thou sawest the iron mixed with miry clay.

**42** And *as* the toes of the feet *were* part of iron, and part of clay, *so* the kingdom shall be partly strong, and partly broken.

**43** And whereas thou sawest iron mixed with miry clay, they shall mingle themselves with the seed of men: but **they shall not cleave one to another, even as iron is not mixed with clay.**

**44** And in the days of these kings shall **the God of heaven set up a kingdom, which shall never be destroyed:** and the kingdom shall not be left to other people, *but* it shall break in pieces and consume all these kingdoms, and it shall stand for ever.

The image seen by the king. Daniel 2:42-43

| BODY PART | METAL | EMPIRE |
|---|---|---|
| HEAD | GOLD | BABYLONIAN |
| CHEST AND ARMS | SILVER | MEDO-PERSIAN |
| HIPS | BRONZE | GREEK |
| LEGS | IRON | ROMAN |
| FEET AND 10 TOES | CLAY AND IRON | FUTURISTIC |

Daniel says ten toes (nations) will not co-exist well. Some believe it to be the EU (European Union) from which the Antichrist will arise. Let's study the rulers during the 400 years.

## PERSIA 536–333 BC

Persia was not harsh with Israel. Although they still ruled the Jews, they allowed them to govern through the high priest. King Cyrus then King Darius sent the Jews back to Israel.

## GREECE 333-323 BC

Alexander the Great, at age 20, set out to conquer the civilized world. He captured Jerusalem but did not destroy it. He even offered sacrifices at the temple. He made the Jews citizens in his cities including Alexander, Egypt. This was the beginning of the pro-Greek feelings among the Jews.

## EGYPT 323-204 BC

When Alexander the Great died, his conquests were divived amongst his four generals; Cassander, Lysimachus, Ptolemy and Selenus. The first Ptolemic king was Ptolemy Soter, king of Egypt. This was the beginning of the Ptolemic dynasty. Ptomemy Soter treated the Jews good. His successor, Ptolemy Philadelphius did likewise. It was during his reign the the Hebrew bible was translated into Greek and became known as the Septuagint. The word Septuagint was used because 70 Jews were sent from Jerusalem to Alexander Egypt to complete the work.

## SYRIA 204-165 BC

Antiochus the Great in (204 BC). invaded Egypt. Judea, and other countries that became part of Syria. Palestine was dived into five sections.

Judea,
Samaria,
Galilee,
Perea,
Trachonitis.

Antiochus Epiphanes (175-164 B.C.) razed Jerusalem destroying the walls, abolishing sacrifices, destroying the Holy of Holies, prohibiting the Jewish religion and sacrificing a pig on the altar. The Temple was rededicated to Jupiter Olympius which was a pagan temple in Rome.

## THE MACCABEAN PERIOD OF INDEPEDENCE 165-63BC

Mattathias had five sons i.e., Judas (Hebrew = the hammer), Simon, Johana, Eleasar and Johnathan. Their surname was Maccabee. They looked at the history of the Jews and said "enough." The cruelty of Antiochus lit their torch.

Judas Maccabeus gathered some troops and had good initial victories. He took back the temple and restored it. It is celebrated today as the Feast of the Dedication. Judas continued having victories.

Antiochus had a son that invaded Judea and defeated Judas Maccabee. It looked like the end for the Maccabees? A self appointed Syrian Regent named Lysias convinces Antiochus's son to make peace with the Maccabees and to restore all religious rights.

Demetrius assumes the Syrian throne. Judas Maccabee was killed and his brother Simon took charge. Like his brother, he won many battles. Peace continued to 63 BC

The books of first and second Maccabeus are contained in the Catholic Apocrypha.

The Roman period was sixty three BC to Christ and beyond to 376AD. Antipater's son Herod, along with the support of the Roman General Pompey, destroyed Jerusalem in 63 BC. Judea was now a providence of Rome. Antipater was appointed Procurator of Judea by Julius Cesar. Antipater appointed his son Herod (age 15) as Governor of Galilee. Sometime later Rome appointed Herod as King of the Jews. He killed three of his wife's brothers, his wife, his mother-in-law and his sons. He was a fratricide fanatic! This is the guy that was king when Jesus was born.

Although the Holy Lands had various rulers, they also encountered new developments during the 400 year period.

Table -1. Contribution; Wikipedia, Sanhedrin.

| SECT | COMMENT |
|------|---------|
| Pharisees | Pharisee in the Greek is "prisha" which means "separated." They were separated to God and strictly observed the law. Their problem was adding to the law. They followed the entire Old Testament and believed in the resurrection. |
| Sadducees | The Sadducees were wealthy aristocrats. They did not believe in the resurrection, angels, the trinity or spirits. They believed that God's law had no part in politics. They followed only the written law and not the oral law. This means they followed the Torah (first five books of Moses) only and none of the rest of the Old Testament. |
| Herodians | They were not a religious group. They were political only and backed the Herods. The Pharisees hated them. Herodians liked the status quo. |

Table 2. Contribution' Wikipedia, Sanhedrin.

| ENTITY | COMMENT |
|--------|---------|
| Scribes | They are sometimes referred to as "lawyers. Their task was to make the law detailed, understandable and able to comply to. |
| Synagogue | The synagogue originated during the captivities. A membership of 10 was required to build one. Jesus frequented them often. The scribes read the scriptures aloud and interpreted them. The intent was not worship, it was instruction. |
| Sanhedrin | The Sanhedrin was the Jewish supreme Court. It was headed by the High Priest. It consisted of scribes, Pharisees, Sadducees and elders. The division of the Sanhedrin is shown next. |

Table 3 THE SANHEDRIN Contribution;
Wikipedia, Sanhedrin.

| TITLE | AMOUNT | COMMENT |
|-------|--------|---------|
| Chief Priests | 24 | Represented 24 orders of the priesthood. |
| Elders | 24 | Heads of famous families. |
| Scribes | 22 | Interpreted the law. |
| TOTAL | 70 | |

FINAL COMMENTS

Why did God wait 400 years? He did it before. Genesis 15:13-16.

> **13** And he said unto Abram, Know of a surety that thy seed shall be a stranger in a land *that is* not theirs, and shall serve them; and they shall afflict them **four hundred years;**

> **14** And also that nation, whom they shall serve, will I judge: and afterward shall they come out with great substance.

**15** And thou shalt go to thy fathers in peace; thou shalt be buried in a good old age.

**16** But in the fourth generation they shall come hither again: **for the iniquity of the Amorites *is* not yet full.**

Why 400 years? The sins (idol worship) of the Amorites had not ripened to the point of punishment. God has a timetable for nations. He gives them a chance to reform. Another reason was that all prophecy had to be fulfilled. Luke 24:44.

**44** And he said unto them, These *are* the words which I spake unto you, while I was yet with you, that **all things must be fulfilled, which were written in the law of Moses, and *in* the prophets, and *in* the psalms, concerning me.**

Some claim there are hundreds of Old Testament prophecies that Christ fulfilled. Space does not allow an analysis of all of them. We will look at the crucifixion.

| OLD TESTAMENT | | NEW TESTAMENT | |
|---|---|---|---|
| PROPHECY | SCRIPTURE | FULFILLED | SCRIPTURE |
| He would be pierced | Zecharia 12:10 | **37** And again another scripture saith, They shall look on him whom they pierced. | John 19:37 |
| He would be given gall | Psalms 69:21 | **34** They gave him vinegar to drink mingled with gall: and when he had tasted *thereof*, he would not drink. | Matthew 27:34 |

| They would not break his legs | Exodus 12:36 | **36** For these things were done, that the scripture should be fulfilled, A bone of him shall not be broken. | John 19:36 |
|---|---|---|---|

We will now look at the methods of execution of the 400 year rulers. Contribution; Wikipedia.

| Persian "Boats" and dichotomy do not match crucifixion. Contribution; Wikipedia, Scalphism – Wikipedia. | "Boats" – This is when two boats, one atop the other, are nailed together with the arms, legs and head extended outside. The boats have holes. A mixture of milk and honey is poured into the victims mouth and smeared onto his extremities and head. His honey excrement and the mixture draws flies, bugs and worms until they devour his body. |
|---|---|
| | Dichotomy – cutting a body into pieces. |
| Egyptian Impalement, burning, beheading nor dichotomy do not match crucifixion. Contribution; Wikipedia; Facts about Ancient Egypt. | Impalement – tied to a post and pierced with a spear or sword. |
| | Burning – thought to destroy the body and prevent eternal life. |
| | Beheading. |
| | Dichotomy - cutting a body into pieces … |
| Hebrews Contribution; Wikipedia; Jewish forms of capital punishment. | Stoning (Sekila) Beheading (Hereg) Strangulation (Chenek) Burning (Serefah) Pouring molten metal down the throat. |
| Roman | Throwing victums off of high places Crucifixion. Contribution; Wikipedia; Ancient Roman. Info., Ancient RomanDeath Penalty. |

It took 500 years for the Romans to show up. They had the execution method that matched the Old Testament prophecies. There are other reasons for the 400 year waiting period. We needed a Herod to slay the Bethlehem boys. We needed a John the Baptist to herald the messiah and we needed a Roman cross.

The Jews entered captivity as a polyestic (worships many Gods) group and came away as a monastic (worship a God) nation. And, they remain so today. However, they allowed Islam to build the Dome of the Rock on the Temple Mount where their temple was destroyed by Rome in 70AD. The only holy place they can offer sacrifices is the temple, not the synagogue. They have not offered sacrifices in almost 2000 years. Jesus replaced the temple with Himself. John 2:19 – 21.

> **19** Jesus answered and said unto them, **Destroy this temple, and in three days I will raise it up.**
>
> **20** Then said the Jews, Forty and six years was this temple in building, and wilt thou rear it up in three days?
>
> **21** But **he spake of the temple of his body.**

Christians are temples. 1 Corinthians 3:16.

> **16** Know **ye not that ye are the temple of God,** and *that* **the Spirit of God dwelleth in you?**

We waited 400 years for Christ to be born. How many more years will we wait until He returns? Only God knows. It has been 2000 years thus far. This we know! God is in control. He knows the hearts of nations and their leaders and how some of them are headed to hell. We do know that we have had 2000 years to proclaim the gospel. How have the nations done? How much will we do with the time we have to go? "We" is not just nations, it is you and I.

# APPENDIX 2

# GOD, GOG AND MAGOG

Ezekiel 38 and 39 tells about Gog (a person) and Magog (a land) confederate with others as they attack Jerusalem in the latter days and are defeated by God. This article identifies the main players and discusses both chapters as events occur. Not all scholars agree on who is who and the sequence of events. Ezekiel was a priest and a major prophet during King Jehoiachin's captivity in Babylon. Let's begin with Noah.

THE NOAH GENEOLOGY - Genesis 10, I Chronicles I.

1 – Noah
    2 – Ham
        3 –**Cush***
4 – Nimrod – founded Calneh in the land of Shinar
4 – Raama
5 – Sheba
5 – Dedan
        3 – **Put** *
    2 – Japheth
        3 – **Gomer** *

4 – Togarmah (Beth Togarmah).

3 – **Magog** * Magog is the land of Gog.

3 – Madai – Iranian Medes

3 – Javan

4 – Tarshish (Tarnish)

3 – **Tubal*** – Gog is their Prince

3 – **Meshech** *– Gog is their prince – ancient name of Moscow

3 – **Tiras*** Gog is their prince

The boldfaced names are those mentioned in Ezekiel 38 or 39. Those containing an asterisk join in the attack on Israel. Noah had three sons, Ham, Seth and Japheth. Ham has four descendants involved in Ezekiel. Japheth has seven. Shem has none. Why? Shem's descendants trace to Abraham and then to Jesus. It was God's plan not to involve the lineage of Jesus in the end time events that occur with Gog and Magog.

1 - Noah

2 – Shem

3 – Arpachshad

4 – Shelah

  5 –Eber

  6 – Peleg

      7 – Reu

      8 – Serug

      9 – Nahor

        10 – Terah

          11 – Abram (Abraham)

            12 – Isaac

              13 – Esau

                13 – Jacob (Israel)

            ↓

            JESUS

We need to learn the meaning of Shinar and Scythians because they are mentioned quite often. Scythians were traveling warriors that lived in wagons. Modern scholars call it the Scythians north of the Black Sea. This is Siberia Russia. Josephus knew them as a nation descended from Magog the <u>Japhetite</u> and explained them to be the "<u>Scythians</u>."

Following are the names/places mentioned in Ezekiel 38 and 39. Citation; Unger's Bible Handbook, Third Edition, 1961, The Moody Bible Institute of Chicago, 1961.

| NAME | COMMENT | LOCATION TODAY |
|---|---|---|
| Gog | Magog is the land north of the Black Sea founded by Japheth. Gog is the Chief Prince of Meshech and Tubal. | Russia |
| DESCENDANTS OF JAPHETH | | |
| Magog | Son of **Japheth.** Founded the Scythians the ancestors of today's Russian people. Called the land of Magog. | Russia |
| Meshek (Meshech) | Son of **Japheth.** Meshek is the ancient name of Moscow. If we draw a line due north from Jerusalem we nearly intersect Moscow. | Moscow |
| Tubal | Son of **Japheth** | Turkey |
| Gomer | Son of **Japheth.** In the Talmud Gomer is spoken of as Germany. Germany was first called "The Land of Gomer." | Eastern Europe Turkey |
| Beth Togamah | Togamah, Son of Gomer the son of **Japheth.** Jewish writers called the Turks Togarmah. | Turkey |
| Tarnish | Son of Javan,. Son of **Japheth** | Spain or England |
| DESCENDANTS OF HAM | | |
| Cush | Son of **Ham.** Cushite is translated Ethiopia or Sudan | Ethiopia or Sudan |
| Put | Son of **Ham** | Libyia |

| Sheba and Dedan | Sons of Raama, the son of Cush, the son of **Ham** | Saudi Arabia |
|---|---|---|
| | OTHERS | |
| Parsa (Persia) | Created by Cyrus the Great in the 6th century BC | Iran |
| The names in the table are those that founded cities/countries. **The attackers are** Russia, Turkey, Iran, Ethiopia or Sudan, Libya, Eastern Europe. | | |

**Those trying to prevent the attack are** Saudi Arabia and Spain or England. Refer to the above as we study Ezekiel 38 and 39 below. Gog or Magog are mentioned in Genesis 10, Ezekiel 38, 39 and Revelation 20.

Some claim that the origin of the attack on Israel emanates from Turkey and not Russia. We need to keep in mind that about 1800 years elapsed from the time of Japheth to Ezekiel. They could have easily migrated. When one reads Genesis, we see where they had a "wonderlust" for travel and creation of cities. God told men over and over again they would create cities. They did not stay where they were born. Ezekiel 38:1-3

> 1 And the word of the LORD came unto me, saying,
>
> 2 Son of man, set thy face against **Gog, the land of Magog, the chief prince of Meshech and Tubal**, and prophesy against him,
>
> 3 And say, Thus saith the Lord GOD; Behold, **I *am* against thee, O Gog**, the **chief prince of Meshech and Tubal:**

Gog is not a king. Remember, Magog is the land of Gog and Gog is the Chief Prince of Meshech (Moscow) and Tubal (Tobolsk). Will Russia and Turkey be in alliance? Moscow's governmental bureaucracy is the President appoints a Prime Minister that is confirmed by the Duma (think of it as the congress). Reference to Gog as the "chief prince" could relate to the Prime Minister? Turkey's bureaucracy is the Prime Minister is the head of government and the President is the Head of State. Reference to Gog could refer to the President?

Moschia is a mountain area of Georgia Russia and the inhabitants are known as the Moschi. They are mentioned in the tablets of Tiglath-Pileser I of Assyria (1115-1100BC) where he fought them in the mountains of Georgia and Armenia. One of the nations in Russia was called the Muscovite Nation. Meshek is an ancient name for Moscow, which is in the region of Muskovy and is on the Moskva river. Tubal could refer to the middle part of Russia, in which is a city named Tobolosk on the Tobol river.

Rhos and Rus have been names used for Western Russia for a millennium. Rosh in Swedish means Russia. This is where the name Russia originated. Rosh, Meshek, and Tubal are all in Ezekiel 38:6 as dwelling "in far north." Ezekiel 38:4-8.

> 4 And I **will turn thee back, and put hooks into thy jaws, and I will bring thee forth**, and all thine army, horses and horsemen, all of them clothed with all sorts *of armour, even* a great company *with* bucklers and shields, all of them handling swords:
>
> 5 **Persia, Ethiopia, and Libya** with them; all of them with shield and helmet:
>
> 6 **Gomer, and all his bands; the house of Togarmah of the north quarters**, and all his bands: *and* many people with thee.

**7** Be thou prepared, and prepare for thyself, thou, and all thy company that are assembled unto thee, and be thou a guard unto them.

**8** After many days thou shalt be visited: **in the latter years** thou shalt come into **the land** *that is* **brought back from the sword**, *and is* gathered out of many people, against the mountains of **Israel,** which have been always waste: but it is brought forth out of the nations, and they shall dwell safely all of them.

What has happened thus far? Gog, in the land of Magog is confederate with Persia (Iran), Ethiopia, Libyia, Gomer (Eastern Europe) and Togarmah to attack "the land that is brought back from the sword" which is Israel. "Brought back from the sword" is return from captivity in the Old Testament and the restoration of Israel after the WWII holocaust. The battle appears in Revelation 20:7-8, just two chapters prior to the end of the bible. This is what meant by "in the latter years'

Why is Israel being attacked? EZ 38:10 says they think an evil thought and verse 12 says they want to take a spoil and a prey. Why pick on Israel? It could be that having a successful campaign against Israel would prove the scriptures to be wrong and dishevel the Judio – Christian communities. It could even be the plan of Russia to occupy Israel. That could lead to dismantling of the temple and more? We know three things; 1) Russia and China are communistic i.e., they do not believe in God. Russia has said that Communism and Region cannot survive together and that one must die. 2) Russia and their counterparts will attack, 3) they will be defeated. Remember, this war occurs after the millennium and Armageddon before the millennium. They are separated by over 1,000 years and are not the same war as some claim. See appendix 5.

The real attackers are not a people or a political system as much as a philosophy. Contribution; Wikipedia, "Is Marxism compatable with the Christian faith?

| SUBJECT | CHRISTIANITY | COMMUNISM |
|---------|-------------|-----------|
| The state | It serves man | Man is a pawn of the state |
| God | God is almighty | The state is almighty |
| God | Serves/glorifies God | God doesn't exist |

Revelation 20:7-8.

> 7 And **when the thousand years are expired, Satan shall be loosed out of his prison,**
>
> 8 And **shall go out to deceive the nations which are in the four quarters of the earth, Gog and Magog**, to gather them together to battle: the number of whom *is* as the sand of the sea.

The "thousand years" is the millennium when Satan is contained and there is peace. The four quarters are North, East, West and South. The first letters of these four words spell NEWS. We must remember that the Old Testament people did not know any NEWS about other countries such as the North and South Americas. God did. Let's return to Ezekiel 38:9-10.

> 9 Thou shalt ascend and come like a storm, thou shalt be like a cloud to cover the land, thou, and all thy bands, and many people with thee.
>
> 10 Thus saith the Lord GOD; It shall also come to pass, *that* at the same time shall things come into thy mind, and **thou shalt think an evil thought:** The devil is at work. Revelation 20:9-10.

Rev 20:9-10

> **9** And they went up on the breadth of the earth, and **compassed the camp of the saints about, and the beloved city: and fire came down from God out of heaven, and devoured them.**

> **10 And the devil that deceived them was cast into the lake of fire and brimstone,** where the beast and the false prophet *are*, and shall be tormented day and night for ever and ever.

Ezekiel 38:11-12.

> 11 And thou shalt say, **I will go up to the land of unwalled villages;** I will go to them that are at rest, that dwell safely, all of them dwelling without walls, and having neither bars nor gates,

> 12 To **take a spoil**, and to **take a prey;** to turn thy hand upon the desolate places that are now inhabited, and upon **the people that are gathered out of the nations**, which have gotten cattle and goods, that dwell in the midst of the land.

The attack occurs after Israel has been gathered from many nations and settled in their country. This happened twice.

1 - during the return from captivity in the Old Testament.

2 - in 1948 under Prime Minister David Ben Gurion (1948-1954) when Jews returned from Hitlers' holocaust.

It will continue as the lost tribes of Israel are gathered back to Israel. It is called diaspora. The "lost tribes" are the ten tribes that formed the Northern Kingdom in the Old Testament. Some claim they are not lost because there are records of some returning to Israel. Some is not all. They went to Assyria then, move to other countries. They are all over the world. NYC USA has millions. Russia has 1.5 million in Moscow. God will regather them into Israel (diaspora) in the end times. The land mass of Israel at that time will be increased six-fold. Not everyone will join the forces of Gog. Ezekiel 38:13-15.

> 13 Sheba, and Dedan, and the merchants of Tarshish, with all the young lions thereof, shall say unto thee, Art thou come to take a spoil? hast thou gathered thy company to take a prey? to carry away silver and gold, to take away cattle and goods, to take a great spoil?

Remember, Sheba and Dan are Saudi Arabia and Tarnish is Spain or England. All are now allies of the USA. Ezekiel 38:14-15.

> 14 Therefore, son of man, prophesy and say unto Gog, Thus saith the Lord GOD; In that day when my people of Israel dwelleth safely, shalt thou not know *it*?

> 15 And thou shalt come from thy place **out of the north parts**, thou, and many people with thee, all of them riding upon horses, **a great company, and a mighty army:**

Horses" was the known transportation for warriors during biblical times so that is what they wrote. The first chapter of Ezekiel tells of his vision of what some call an aircraft. Others call it a UFO. In 1901 a Baptist Minister Burrell Cannon of Coffeeville, Mississippi designed and built his Ezekiel Airship as described by Ezekiel. It flew before the Wright brother's flight.

Ezekiel 38:6 says Gog's armies will come from the "north quarters" This could include China? Associated Press Release April 24, 1964 estimated that China has 200,000,000 armed militiamen. The bible says the sixth angel sounds his trumpet and releases four angels from the Euphrates to lead an army of 200,000,000 to kill one third of men. The world's population is estimated at 9 billion. 1/3 = 3 billion. We should note that the four that were released are demonic angels. God is punishing the people. If we slap Him, He can slap back. Ask Noah!

Revelation 9:16.

> 16 And the number of the army of the horsemen *were* **two hundred thousand thousand:** and I heard the number of them.

"Two hundred thousand thousand = 200,000 x 1,000 = 200,000,000,. The population of China in 2015 was 1,376,049,000 people. That means less than 15% of the population is in the military. That is a doable do! Ez 38:16.

> 16 And thou shall come up against my people of Israel, as a cloud to cover the land; **it shall be in the latter days,** and I will bring thee against my land, that the heathen may know me, when I shall be sanctified in thee, O Gog, before their eyes.

Ezekiel 38:17-18.

> 17 Thus saith the Lord GOD; *Art* thou he of whom **I have spoken in old time by my servants the prophets of Israel**, which prophesied in those days *many* years that I would bring thee against them?

18 And it shall come to pass at the same time when **Gog shall come** against the land of Israel, saith the Lord GOD, *that* my fury shall come up in my face.

"Furry"! Oh! Oh! God is angry. Ezekiel 38:19-20.

**19** For in my jealousy *and* in the fire of my wrath have I spoken, Surely in that day there **shall be a great shaking in the land of Israel;**

**20** So that the fishes of the sea, and the fowls of the heaven, and the beasts of the field, and all creeping things that creep upon the earth, and all the men that *are* upon the face of the earth, shall shake at my presence, and **the mountains shall be thrown down, and the steep places shall fall, and every wall shall fall to the ground.** This is beginning to sound like H-Bombs? How many H bombs would it take to destroy Israel? We need to know the size of Israel.

ISRAEL COMPARED TO NEW JERSEY.
Contribution; Wikipedia, Israel compared to New Jersey."

| SUBJECT | LENGTH | WIDTH | POPULATION |
|---------|--------|-------|------------|
| New Jersey | 166 miles | 70 miles | 8,000,000 |
| Israel | 290 miles | 85 miles | 6,000,000 |

Because Israel and New Jersey are similar in size and population, we can ask how many bombs it would take to eliminate New Jersey. One! Israel is not concerned with defense as much as they are with existence.

Contribution; Wikipedia, Dmitry Pavlov (general) – Wilipedia. Russian General Dmitry Pavlov photographed a soviet H Bomb test in the arctic and reported the following:

> "All the **mountains** on the blast site **were just deleted** and the land was **leveled** as if someone wanted to make of the island a smooth skating surface. Everything that was in a range of 25 km from the blast zone, **disappeared** from the earth as if it just evaporated."

25KM = a little more than4 40 miles. That is not the only damage that occurs. Radiation clouds float throughout the globe causing cancer and mutations. It is doubtful that Jerusalem (1mile x 6 miles) would be bombed because the Dome of the Rock (Muslim) is located there. The rest of Israel is up for grabs. Compounding this problem is the capability of Israel to respond within one minute to fire a bomb at Tehran, Iran killing millions. Other major powers would join the bombing leading to elimination of the human race. Russia and the USA each have over ten thousand of them. Ez 38:21.

> 21 And I will call for a sword against him throughout all my mountains, saith the Lord GOD: **every man's sword shall be against his brother.**

This reads like inner-fighting among the troops? Ez 38:22.

> 22 And I will plead against him with pestilence and with blood; and **I will rain upon him**, and upon his bands, and upon the many people that *are* with him, **an overflowing rain, and great hailstones, fire, and brimstone.**

Revelation 16:21.

21 And there fell upon men a great **hail out of heaven,** *every stone* **about the weight of a talent:** and men blasphemed God because of the plague of the hail; for the plague thereof was exceeding great.

A talent in the Hebrew measure is 93 pounds. Years ago, the author experienced a hail storm larger than golf balls. Local car dealers had a "hail sale" due to damage. Had the hail weighed 93 pounds the cars would have been totaled. Let's introduce a bit of comedy. 2 Sam 12:29-30.

**29** And David gathered all the people together, and went to Rabbah, and fought against it, and took it.

30 And **he took their king's crown from off his head, the weight whereof was a talent of gold with the precious stones: and it was set on David's head.** And he brought forth the spoil of the city in great abundance.

Doesn't seem like much except a talent (93 pounds and, that is just the jewels) is the approximate equivalent of three cinder blocks. How does one wear a 100 pound hat? If he stood up, it could break his neck or cause a hernia.

Ezekiel 38:23

23 Thus will I magnify myself, and sanctify myself; and I will be known in the eyes of many nations, and they shall know that I *am* the LORD.

This is reminiscent of what God said when he drown the Egyptians in the Reds Sea during the Exodus. Exodus 14:17-18.

17 And I, behold, I will harden the hearts of the Egyptians, and they shall follow them: and I will get me honour upon Pharaoh, and upon all his host, upon his chariots, and upon his horsemen.

18 And **the Egyptians shall know that I** *am* **the LORD**, when I have gotten me honour upon Pharaoh, upon his chariots, and upon his horsemen.

Ezekiel 38:17-23 – Gog's armies are severely defeated. God promises a mighty shaking in the land of Israel. Mountains shall be thrown down, cliffs shall tumble, and walls shall crumble. This sounds like the results of H-bombs? Gog's armies shall fight against themselves in mortal combat. This may indicate that some may not have agreed with the attack strategy or even attacking at all so, they rebelled.

THIS IS THE END OF EZEKIEL 38

Ezekiel 39:1-29.

1 Therefore, thou son of man, prophesy against Gog, and say, Thus saith the Lord GOD; Behold, I *am* against thee, O Gog, the chief prince of Meshech and Tubal:

We notice that this verse carries the same words as Ezekiel 38:3. Some scholars claim there are two separate invasions. However, Ezekiel 39 deals with a "clean-up operation whereas Ezekiel 38 deals with the attack.

2 **And I will turn thee back, and leave but the sixth part of thee**, and will cause thee to come up

from the north parts, and will bring thee upon the mountains of Israel:

3 And I will smite thy bow out of thy left hand, and will cause thine arrows to fall out of thy right hand.

4 Thou shalt fall **upon the mountains** of Israel, thou, and all thy bands, and the people that *is* with thee: I will give thee unto the ravenous birds of every sort, and *to* the beasts of the field to be devoured.

5 Thou shalt fall **upon the open field:** for I have spoken *it*, saith the Lord GOD.

6 And **I will send a fire on Magog**, and among them that dwell carelessly in the isles: and they shall know that I *am* the LORD.

When God said "I will but leave a sixth part of thee. He is also saying that He will turn back 83.3% of the attacking forces. Now He will deal with 16.7% of them. Scripture does not say what turned them back. Perhaps it is a threat of involvement by another country? "I will send a fire on Magog" may be the answer? Remember, Magog is the land of Gog and Gog is the Chief Prince of Meshech (Moscow) and Tubal (Tobolsk). It could possibly be that a third country bombed Russia?

7 So will I make my holy name known in the midst of my people Israel; and I will not *let them* pollute my holy name any more: and **the heathen shall know that I *am* the LORD, the Holy One in Israel.**

8 Behold, **it is come, and it is done**, saith the Lord GOD; this *is* the day whereof I have spoken.

9 And they that dwell in the cities of Israel shall go forth, and shall **set on fire and burn the weapons**, both the shields and the bucklers, the bows and the arrows, and the handstaves, and the spears, and **they shall burn them with fire seven years:**

10 So that they shall take no wood out of the field, neither cut down *any* out of the forests; for they shall burn the weapons with fire: and they shall **spoil those that spoiled them**, and **rob those that robbed them**, saith the Lord GOD.

"Burn the weapons" doesn't sound like an H Bomb. Verse 10 sounds like God is applying "an eye for an eye" and "a tooth for a tooth" legacy of the Old Testament.

11 And it shall come to pass in that day, *that* **I will give unto Gog a place there of graves in Israel, the valley of the passengers on the east of the sea:** and **it shall stop the *noses* of the passengers**: and there shall they bury Gog and all his multitude: and they shall call *it* The valley of Hamon Gog. Passengers in the Hebrew is "idabar" which means "to passover." It appears that this is an area where people just traveled through it on their way to another place. It sounds remote. "East of the sea" is east of the Dead Sea.

12 And **seven months shall the house of Israel be burying of them,** that they may cleanse the land.

13 Yea, **all the people of the land shall bury *them*;** and it shall be to them a renown the day that I shall be glorified, saith the Lord GOD.

14 And they shall sever out men of continual employment, passing through the land to bury with the passengers those that remain upon the face of the earth, to cleanse it: after the end of seven months shall they search.

15 And the passengers *that* pass through the land, when *any* seeth a man's bone, then shall he set up a sign by it, till the buriers have buried it in the valley of Hamongog.

16 **And also the name of the city *shall be* Hamonah.** Thus shall they cleanse the land.

Let's discussed what happened from verse 11 to 16. They are given the Valley of the passengers on the east side of the Dead Sea that they will call Hamongog which in Hebrew is means "multitude of Gog." It is near the city of Homanoh which, in Hebrew means "multitude." The stench will be great. They will have a full time crew looking for the dead for 7 years and any bones flagged by anyone.

17 And, thou son of man, thus saith the Lord GOD; **Speak unto every feathered fowl, and to every beast of the field, Assemble yourselves, and come; gather yourselves on every side to my sacrifice** that I do sacrifice for you, *even* a great sacrifice upon the mountains of Israel, that ye may eat flesh, and drink blood.

18 Ye shall eat the flesh of the mighty, and drink the blood of the princes of the earth, of rams, of lambs, and of goats, of bullocks, all of them fatlings of Bashan.

Bashan is a district east of the Jordon River and east of the Dead Sea.

19 And ye shall eat fat till ye be full, and drink blood till ye be drunken, of my sacrifice which I have sacrificed for you.

20 Thus ye shall be filled at my table with horses and chariots, with mighty men, and with all men of war, saith the Lord GOD.

21 And I will set my glory among the heathen, and all the heathen shall see my judgment that I have executed, and my hand that I have laid upon them.

Verses 17 – 21 says the wildlife is going to feast on the bodies of Gog's army.

22 So the house of Israel shall know that I *am* the LORD their God from that day and forward.

23 **And the heathen shall know that the house of Israel went into captivity for their iniquity:** because they trespassed against me, therefore hid I my face from them, and gave them into the hand of their enemies: so fell they all by the sword.

Captivity refers to the Old Testament captivities of Israel and Judah.

24 According to their uncleanness and according to their transgressions have I done unto them, and hid my face from them.

25 Therefore thus saith the Lord GOD; **Now will I bring again the captivity of Jacob, and have mercy upon the whole house of Israel**, and will be jealous for my holy name;

Jacob and Israel are the same person. In Genesis 32:28 Jacob's name is changed to Israel. The "house of Israel" refers to all of the Jews.

26 After that they have borne their shame, and all their trespasses whereby they have trespassed against me, when they dwelt safely in their land, and none made *them* afraid.

27 When I have brought them again from the people, and gathered them out of their enemies' lands, and am sanctified in them in the sight of many nations;

28 Then shall they know that I *am* the LORD their God, which caused them to be led into captivity among the heathen: but I have gathered them unto their own land, and have left none of them any more there.

29 Neither will I hide my face any more from them: for I have poured out my spirit upon the house of Israel, saith the Lord GOD.

# THIS IS THE END OF EZEKIEL 39

God is simply saying that the Jews have learned their lesson and by the empowering of his spirit, he will not forsake them again if they respond to the Holy Spirit.

Revelation 20:11-15.

> 11 And I saw a **great white throne**, and him that sat on it, from whose face the earth and the heaven fled away; and there was found no place for them.

> 12 And I saw the dead, small and great, stand before God; and the books were opened: and **another book was opened, which is *the book* of life**: and the dead were judged out of those things which were written in the books, according to their works.

> 13 And the sea gave up the dead which were in it; and death and hell delivered up the dead which were in them: and they were judged every man according to their works.

> 14 And death and hell were cast into the lake of fire. This is the second death.

> 15 And **whosoever was not found written in the book of life was cast into the lake of fire.**

Verse 10 says goodby to Satan forever. The key phrase here is "the book of life." How does one get their name in the book? This is a critical question because if our name is missing, we join Satan in hell forever. It also applies to the Jews.

Daniel 12:1-2.

**1** And at that time shall Michael stand up, the great prince which standeth for the children of thy people: and **there shall be a time of trouble, such as never was** since there was a nation *even* to that same time: and at that time **thy people shall be delivered, every one that shall be found written in the book.**

**2** And many of them that sleep in the dust of the earth shall awake, some to everlasting life, and some to shame *and* everlasting contempt.

It appears that the Old Testament had a Book of Life although they didn't call it that.

## WHEN WILL GOG ATTACK ISRAEL?

Some say that Revelation 20:8 is symbolic of all evil world powers attacking Israel. If that were true, why not say so? Why bring Gog and Magog into it? Ezekiel 38 and 39 does not say when Israel is attacked but Rev20:7-10 does.

**7** And **when the thousand years are expired, Satan shall be loosed out of his prison,**

**8** And shall go out to **deceive the nations** which are in the four quarters of the earth, **Gog and Magog, to gather them together to battle:** the number of whom *is* as the sand of the sea.

**9** And they went up on the breadth of the earth, and compassed the camp of the saints about, and **the**

**beloved city:** and fire came down from God out of heaven, and devoured them.

**10** And the devil that deceived them was cast into the lake of fire and brimstone, where the beast and the false prophet *are*, and shall be tormented day and night for ever and ever

Gog unites many nations against Israel, targeting Jerusalem. This will happen after the millennium. As soon as satan is unbound, he gets Gog active to attack Israel. Who are Israel's current enemies?

Contribution; Wikipedia; These 36 Countries Don't Recognize Israel – Brilliant Maps.

| NEVER HAD RELATIONS WITH ISRAEL (21) | BROKE RELATIONS WITH ISRAEL (15) |
|---|---|
| 1. Afghanistan | 1. Bahrain (1996–2000; Second Intifada) |
| 2. Algeria | 2. Bolivia (1950–2009; Gaza War) |
| 3. Bangladesh | 3. Chad (1960–1972; solidarity with the Palestinians) |
| 4. Bhutan | 4. Cuba (1950–1973; Yom Kippur War) |
| 5. Brunei | 5. Guinea (1959–1967; unknown but presumable related to 1967 Arab-Israeli war) |
| 6. Comoros | 6. Iran (1948–1951, 1953–1979; Islamic revolution in Iran) |
| 7. Djibouti | 7. Mali (1960–1973; pressure from neighboring countries) |
| 8. Indonesia | 8. Morocco (1994–2000; Second Intifada) |
| 9. Iraq | 9. Mauritania (2000–2009; Gaza War) |
| 10. Kuwait | 10. Nicaragua (1948–1982, 1992–2010; Gaza flotilla raid) |
| 11. Lebanon | 11. Niger (1960–1973, 1996–2002; Second Intifada) |
| 12. Libya | 12. Oman (1996–2000; Second Intifada) |

| 13. Malaysia | 13. Qatar (1996–2009; Gaza War) |
|---|---|
| 14. North Korea | 14. Tunisia (1996–2000; Second Intifada) |
| 15. Pakistan | 15. Venezuela (1950–2009 |
| 16. Saudi Arabia | |
| 17. Somalia | |
| 18. Sudan | |
| 19. Syria | |
| 20. United Arab Emirates | |
| 21. Yemen | |

| NOTES | Hezbollah was founded by Iran to continue Lebanon border disputes with Israel. |
|---|---|
| | Hamas wants to replace Israel with a Palestinian state and has waged war with Israel since 1987, notably by suicide attacks. |
| | The PLO (Palestine Liberation Organization) says the Zionists (Jews) unjustly expelled the Palestinians. They want the land back including Israel. |
| | Al-Qaeda has called for all Muslims to kill Jews and Americans. They want to recover Jerusalem. |

## FINAL COMMENT

Did you notice how many of the nations in the above table are Muslim and how they surround Israel? Luke 21:20.

**20 And when ye shall see Jerusalem compassed with armies, then know that the desolation thereof is nigh.**

A main rift between the Jews and the Muslims is The Dome of the Rock or Mosque of Omar. It is an Islamic structure built on The Temple Mount in Jerusalem where the Jews' temple stood. The dome was built in 691AD, collapsed in 1015 and was rebuilt in 1023 by the Muslims. They claim that Mohammad ascended to heaven from this spot on his horse Barak. They also state that there would be a war should the Jews try to remove it. There are 1.3 billion Muslims that comprise 1/4 of the world's population. Israel has 6,000,000 Jews and wouldn't stand a chance. However, in recent years both Russia and the USA were contacted by Israel to help build the next temple.

The Jewish temple was destroyed by the Romans in 70AD. The Jews believe this is the place where God created the universe and where Abram tried to sacrifice his son Isaac. Jews could only offer sacrifices in the Tabernacle or the temple. Why didn't they rebuild it after Rome destroyed it in 70AD? They tried! In 362 AD, emperor Julian ordered Alypius of Antioch to rebuild it. In 363 an earthquake ruined the foundation. When Julian died, so did the effort to rebuild the temple. It seems that God only wanted the Jews to build the temple and not a foreign power. They missed their open window when the Maccabean brothers gave Israel a 102 year period of independence from Rome spanning 165BC – 63BC. About 2,000 years have passed and no temple.

Israel has had some recent victories via its prime ally, the USA.

1 – President Thrump has moved the USA embassy from Tel-Aviv to Jerusalem.

2 – The USA President Trump recognized Israel's sovereignty over the disputed Golan Heights.

3 – Prime Minister Benjamin Netanylhu was reelected for the fifth term

4 – The President of Sudan, Omar aL Bashir, was ousted and arrested after a brutal 30 year reign. He is reported to be responsible for 300,000 deaths in the Darfar region.

5 – There are murmurings that Putin and Thrump have made secret arrangement for Israel to build the temple. Muslims may think

twice before attacking the two top world powers? The Mid-east is changing by the hour.

The Dome of the Rock is a Muslim structure in Jerusalem, God's Holy City. Should Israel decide to eliminate it, could that trigger the events in Ezekiel 38 and 39? The Jews need not think that God is going to defeat Gog and all of them will go to heaven. In Ezekiel 39:29 God said "**I have poured out my spirit upon the house of Israel.**" This is the Holy Spirit. Scripture tells us that the Holy Spirit convicts us of sin and invites us to confess Jesus as our savior. How do we respond to the Holy Spirit and receive Jesus as our savior?

Read this: Romans 3:23 For all have sinned and fall short of the glory of God.

Romans 6:23 For the wages of sin is death, but the gift of God is eternal life in Christ Jesus our Lord.

Romans 5:8 But God demonstrates his love for us while we were still sinners Jess died for us.

Pray this: "Please forgive me of my sins and help me not to sin. I believe in Jesus as your son as my Lord and savior and that he died for my sins. Thank you and help me to stay close to you and grow in the Christian faith. Amen."

If you prayed this prayer, welcome aboard. You have a one way first class non-stop flight to heaven where your name is written in The Book of Life. Enjoy your flight.

# APPENDIX 3

# DIVISION OF THE LAND (EZ 48), THOSE SEALED (REV 7), ASSIGNED GATES

Ezekiel chapter 48, details how the land will be divided among the tribes. The following table details how the land was divided plus each tribe's mentioned in Revelation 7 and the gates assigned to them. Omissions are boldfaced and explained later. Shown next is the division of the land among the 12 tribes (Ez 48), those sealed, Rev 7, assigned Gates.

| EZEKIEL 48 | REVELATION 7 | GATES |
|---|---|---|
| Dan – Verses 1, 32 | NM | East Gate |
| Judah – Verse 7, | 12,000 sealed Judah - Verse 5 | North Gate |
| Rueben – Verses 6, 31 | 12,000 sealed Rueben - Verse 5 | North Gate |
| Gad – Verses 27, 34 | 12,000 sealed Gad -Verse 5 | West Gate |
| Asher – Verses 2,33 | 12,000 sealed Asher – Verse 6 | West Gate |
| Naphtali – Verses 3, 34 | 12,000 sealed Naphtali - Verse 6 | West Gate |
| Manasseh –Verse 4 | 12,000 Manasseh – Verse 6. First son of Joseph | NM |
| Ephraim – Verse 5 | **NM** Second son of Joseph | NM |

| Simeon – Verses 24, 33 | 12,000 sealed Simeon – Verse 7 | South Gate |
|---|---|---|
| Sons of Zadok Verse 11 | 12,000 sealed Levi - Verse 7 | North Gate |
| Issachar – Verses 25,33 | 12,000 sealed Issachar – Verse 7 | South Gate |
| Zebulun – Verses 26, 33 | 12,000 sealed Zebulun – Verse 8 | South Gate |
| Joseph – **NM** | 12,000 sealed Joseph - Verse 8 | East Gate |
| Benjamin – Verses 23, 32 | 12,000 sealed Benjamin – Verse 8 | East Gate |
| TOTAL 12 | 12 | 12 |
| NOTES | | |
| Ephraim was the son of Joseph. His mother was Asenath, daughter of an Egyptian priest named Potiphera who served the Sun God Ra. Ephraim was born in Egypt. | | |
| Mannasseh was the son of Joseph. His mother is unknown. He was born in Egypt. | | |
| **NM** = Not Mentioned | | |

Let's research the boldfaced entries in the above table and try to explain what happened and why. We will start with Dan. Joshua 19:40-48.

Dan was the last to inherit land consisting of 18 cities (Joshua 19:40-48). His land was in the far north and on the Mediterranean Sea. The tribe of Dan was the second largest at 62,700 (Num 1:39). Judah was the largest. The 18 cities were not large enough so Dan conquered Laiah. God did not give it to him. He took it. This is recorded in Judges 18:1-31. It begins with Dan sending out spies for more land. They met a priest that had been hired by Micah. They then went to the city of Laish and found it easy to conquer. They found an ephod, a graven Image and a teraphim, which is an image or idol. An ephod is a breastplate worn by a priest. They talked a young priest into serving the tribe of Dan instead of his current employer, Micah. They attacked the city of Laish and burnt it to the ground. Dan got his nineteenth city. They rebuilt it and named it Dan. They set up the image and worshiped it. Was Dan punished by God because he captured a city that was not given to him by Joshua and worshiped a graven image? It should be obvious why Dan is not listed in Revelation 7 and did not have 12,000 sealed. He left God for idols and God left him with his idols. He worshipped Egypt's Golden Calf as did Bethel in the south.

Next are Manasseh and Ephraim. In order to understand what happened and why, we need to reproduce a portion of the above table.

**NM** = Not mentioned.

| EZEKIEL 48 | REVELATION 7 | GATES |
|---|---|---|
| Manasseh – verse 4 | Manasseh - verse 6 12,000 sealed. First son of Joseph | NM |
| Ephraim – verse 5 | **NM** Second son of Joseph | NM |
| Joseph – **NM** | Joseph - verse 8 12,000 sealed | East |

Ephraim got land but nothing else. Why did he get land? Ezekiel 47:13.

> **13** Thus saith the Lord GOD; This *shall be* the border, whereby ye shall inherit the land according to the twelve tribes of Israel: **Joseph *shall have two* portions.**

Josephs two portions went to his sons Manasseh and Ephraim. Joseph didn't get any land. The mother of both sons was an Egyptian that Joseph married.

Why didn't Manasseh and Ephraim have a gate named after them? It was a trade-off i.e., the sons got the land and their father Joseph got the gate. Had the sons been given a gate that would equate to a total of 14 tribes when there were just 12.

Why wasn't Ephraim listed in Revelation 7 and given 12,000 sealed? Perhaps it was because of his mother? Ephraim's mother was Asenath, daughter of an Egyptian priest Potiphera who served the Sun God Ra. This was the top God of Egypt. Did some of this stick with Ephraim? Exodus 20:3 is the first commandment.

> **3 Thou shalt have no other gods before me.**

We must note that if Ephraim had been given a gate that would have equated to 13 tribes when there were just 12 tribes.

The next question is, who is the prince mentioned in Ezekiel? Prince in the Hebrew is "nasi" meaning "lifted up or exalted" Notice that he is not Jesus because he prepares a sin offering in Ezekiel 45:22 and 46:4, 12 and has children in Ezekiel 46:16. Ezekiel identified the prince in 34:24, 37:25.

> 24 And I the LORD will be their God, and my servant **David a prince among them;** I the LORD have spoken it.
>
> 25 And they shall dwell in the land that I have given unto Jacob my servant, wherein your fathers have dwelt; and they shall dwell therein, even they, and their children, and their children's children for ever: and my servant **David shall be their prince for ever.**

We realize that the above activities occur after the end of the Great Tribulation and the return of Christ. The Jews get their promised land on earth and ruled the earth. The Christians are in the New Jerusalem which is a 1500 mile cube in space.

# APPENDIX 4

# ARMAGEDDON

There are many interpretations of Armageddon. Some claim Armageddon and the Gog/Magog conflicts are the same? This cannot be true as shown in Appendix 5.

Armageddon (Har Magedon) occurs between the pouring out of the 6th and 7th vials (bowls) of Rev 16. The 7th vial ends the Great Tribulation and Daniels 70th week. We are ready for Christ to return and begin the millennium. After the 1,000 year millennium satan is loosed and immediately invokes the Gog/Magog war. Therefore, Armageddon is prior to the 1,000 year millennium and the Gog/Magog is after the millennium. There are separated by at least 1,000 years. The word "Armegeddon" only appears in Rev 16:16. It means Mount of Megiddo but the war occurs in the adjacent southern plain of Esdraelon (Jezrael) which is 36 x 15 miles or 540 square miles.

Armageddon is a pile of defeated cities and not a plain. Each time a city was captured, it was leveled, buried and a new city built on top of it. Megiddo has 26 levels of buried cities topping out at about 70 feet high. Israel captured the fifth level. The mound covers about 13 acres

Revelation chapter 16 contains the whole story. It describes the 7 vials and Armageddon. Armageddon occurs between the 6th and 7th vials. The 6th vial describes how John saw evil spirits shaped like frogs come out of the mouth of the evil trinity. Their task was Rev 16:12-14.

> 12 And the sixth angel poured out his vial upon the great river Euphrates; and the water thereof was dried up, that the way of the kings of the east might be prepared.
>
> 13 And I saw three unclean spirits like frogs come out of the mouth of the dragon, and out of the mouth of the beast, and out of the mouth of the false prophet.
>
> 14 For they are the spirits of devils, working miracles, which go forth unto the kings of the earth and of the whole world, to gather them to the battle of that great day of God Almighty.

Verse 12 says the River Euphrates was dried up to allow Armies from the east to join the war. Verse 14 says the evil spirits are to gather kings throughout the world to attack Israel. The war was to occur in verse Rev 16:16.

> 16 And he gathered them together into a place called in the Hebrew tongue Armageddon.

Some have claimed that Armageddon and the Gog/Magog wars are the same. See appendix 5.

# APPENDIX 5

# DIFFERENCES BETWEEN THE GOG/ MAGOG AND THE ARMAGEDDON WARS

| SUBJECT | GOG/MAGOG EZ 38-39 Rev 20:7-8 | ARMAGEDDON Rev 16:16-21 |
|---------|-------------------------------|-------------------------|
| Bones | Buries the bones (radioactive?). | No mention of bones. |
| The army | They die in the northern mountains and never reach Israel. | The army reaches the valley of Jehoshaphat |
| Peace and safety. | Israel is at peace and safe when they are attacked. | Israel has already fled from antichrist and are hiding. |
| Nations | Some are not involved. | All nations are involved. |

| Spiritual figures. | No mention of them. | The beast, antichrist and the false prophet reign. The beast and the false prophet were thrown into the Lake of Fire at the start of the millennium and preceded satan by 1,000 years. They were not available for the Gog/Magog war. |
|---|---|---|
| Survival | 1/6 survive. | All of the army is destroyed. |
| Purpose | Bring Israel to repentance. | Deliver Israel from the beast. |
| Signs | No prior signs given. | Occurs after sign in the sky and on earth. |
| Mentioned in scripture. | Rev 20:8. Satan was loosed after the millennium. | Rev 16:14 - 16. The battle of that great day of God Almighty. |

The city is a 13 acre mound 70 feet high and is known as Tel-el-Mutesellim. Armageddon mean "Hill of Meggido" which is 70 feet high. This is equivalent to a 7 story building. There is about 6 acres per side or 1200 feet (4 football fields). Not too big but, really high. Why? The city had been captured 26 times. The custom was to bury the captured city. This happened 26 times. How does one capture such a city? Cut off their water supply and starve them out. The only residents are 847 holocaust survivors from 1945. As of 2020, their average age was at least 85.

I personally believe that the amount slain per nation will be dependent on the severity of their sins. For example, The USA has heard the gospel many times. Unlike some countries, there are churches everywhere. We have not only legalize but have government support for abortion, gays, same sex marriage, transgenders, sodomy, and more. We have slapped God in the face after He has blessed us so much and He will slap back.

Keep in mind that battle of Armageddon occurs during the Great Tribulation and the Gog/Magog war occurs 1,000 years after the Millennium. They are over 1,000 years apart.

# APPENDIX 6

# GOD BRINGS THE DEAD SEA TO LIFE

## THE SPIRITUAL VIEW

Our text is Ezekiel 47. Verses 1 – 12 addresses water and 13 – 23 addresses land where the 12 tribes each inherit a portion. We will study verses 1 – 12. Some scholars claim they are symbolic of salvation while others take them literally. We will look at both views. Ezekiel 47:1-12

| | SYMBOLIC VIEW | |
|---|---|---|
| VERSE | SCRIPTURE | COMMENT |
| 1 | **1** Afterward he brought me again unto the door of the house; and, behold, waters issued out from under the threshold of the house eastward: for the forefront of the house *stood toward* the east, and the waters came down from under from the right side of the house, at the south *side* of the altar. | Waters come from under the altar in the temple and flow eastward. The temple is God. The altar is Jesus. The waters are the gospel and contain those that are saved. This is the beginning of Christianity. |

| | | |
|---|---|---|
| 2 | **2** Then brought he me out of the way of the gate northward, and led me about the way without unto the utter gate by the way that looketh eastward; and, behold, there ran out waters on the right side. | Water is the gospel. Notice that we looked eastward towards the Dead Sea. |
| 3 | **3** And when the man that had the line in his hand went forth eastward, he measured a thousand cubits, and he brought me through the waters; the waters *were* to the ankles. | In 1500 feet the water is 6 inches deep. The gospel had just begun to be preached and some were saved. |
| 4 | **4** Again he measured a thousand, and brought me through the waters; the waters *were* to the knees. Again he measured a thousand, and brought me through; the waters *were* to the loins. | Another 1500 feet and the water is 3 feet. More gospel, more saved. |
| 5 | **5** Afterward he measured a thousand; *and it was* a river that I could not pass over: for the waters were risen, waters to swim in, a river that could not be passed over. | Another 1500 feet. Total is now 4500 feet or more than ¾ mile. The water is about 7 feet high. More gospel., More savred. It is going to travel 12 miles to the Dead Sea. Christianity is in full bloom. |
| 6 | **6** And he said unto me, Son of man, hast thou seen *this*? Then he brought me, and caused me to return to the brink of the river | Do Christians realize how the early gospel has spread? |
| 7 | **7** Now when I had returned, behold, at the bank of the river *were* very many trees on the one side and on the other. | The water (gospel) brings life. God sustains all life. |

| | | |
|---|---|---|
| 8 | **8** Then said he unto me, These waters issue out toward the east country, and go down into the desert, and go into the sea: *which being* brought forth into the sea, the waters shall be healed. | The Dead Sea represents eternity. Christians are pouring in. The healed Dead Sea represents a pure heaven. |
| 9 | **9** And it shall come to pass, *that* every thing that liveth, which moveth, whithersoever the rivers shall come, shall live: and there shall be a very great multitude of fish, because these waters shall come thither: for they shall be healed; and every thing shall live whither the river cometh. | The water (gospel) brings life and healing. Whatever it touches is healed. |
| 10 | **10** And it shall come to pass, *that* the fishers shall stand upon it from Engedi even unto Eneglaim; they shall be a *place* to spread forth nets; their fish shall be according to their kinds, as the fish of the great sea, exceeding many. | The Dead Sea will have plenty of fish as will heaven have plenty of Christians. There will be a variety of people. |
| 11 | **11** But the miry places thereof and the marishes thereof shall not be healed; they shall be given to salt. | Remember, the Dead Sea represents eternity. The marshes are hell. |

| 12 | 12 And by the river upon the bank thereof, on this side and on that side, shall grow all trees for meat, whose leaf shall not fade, neither shall the fruit thereof be consumed: it shall bring forth new fruit according to his months, because their waters they issued out of the sanctuary: and the fruit thereof shall be for meat, and the leaf thereof for medicine. | The gospel sustains us. It feeds and heals. |
|---|---|---|
| NONE | Revelations mentions a river | Revelation 22:1-2<br><br>**1** And he shewed me **a pure river of water of life, clear as crystal, proceeding out of the throne of God and of the Lamb.**<br><br>**2** In the midst of the street of it, and on either side of the river, *was there* the tree of life, which bare twelve *manner of* fruits, *and* yielded her fruit every month: and the leaves of the tree *were* for the healing of the nations. |

| NONE | Joel talked about the river. | Joel 3:18 |
|------|------|------|
| | | 18 And it shall come to pass in that day, *that* the mountains shall drop down new wine, and the hills shall flow with milk, and all the rivers of Judah shall flow with waters, and **a fountain shall come forth of the house of the LORD,** and shall water the valley of Shittim.<br><br>NOTE – Shittim is near Jordan. |
| NONE | Zachariah talked about the river | Zachariah 14:28<br><br>**8** And it shall be in that day, *that* living waters shall go out from Jerusalem; half of them toward the former sea, and half of them toward the hinder sea: in summer and in winter shall it be. The former sea is the Mediterranean Sea and the hinder sea: is the Dead Sea. This is discussed in Appendix 8 |

# GOD BRINGS THE DEAD SEA TO LIFE
## THE LITERAL VIEW

We need to know some information about the Dead Sea so we can better interpret scripture.

1 – It is known in the Bible as the "Salt Sea" or the "Sea of the Arabah."

2 – It is bordered by Jordan to the east and Israel to the west.

3 - At 1412 feet below sea level it is the lowest spot on earth. The water is about 1300 feet deep in the north and 20 feet in the south.

4 - 10 times as salty as the ocean and 2 times as salty as the Salt Lake in Utah.

5 – It is 31 miles long and 9 miles wide. It is more a lake than a sea.

6 – Due to the modern diversion of the Jordan river for industrial and other purposes, the water level is decreasing about 5 - 8 feet per year and the salt and mineral contents increasing. It is getting deader! That means the lowest point on earth is getting even lower.

7 – It is fed by the Jordon river in the north and five smaller streams. The streams flow through nitrous soils and sulfurous springs. The

Jordon River empties into the Sea of Galilee which, in turn, empties into the Dead Sea.

8 – There is no outlet, nor will ever be one. Following is an illustration of the major fault lines (see arrows) running through the Kidron Valley and splitting the Dead Sea from north to south. "A" is The Mount of Olives and "B": is The Temple Mount. Wintry water flows through the Kidron Valley (about 20 miles long) and drops some 3,900 feet through a seventy mile journey into a Dead Sea gorge about 1,200 feet deep. The Jordan Rift Valley is another fault splitting the Dead Sea from east to west.

The following table details the literal approach and lists Ezekiel 47 by verse and scripture followed by comments.

| VERSE | SCRIPTURE |
|---|---|
| 1 | Afterward he brought me again unto the door of the **house;** and, behold, waters issued out from under the threshold of the house eastward: for the forefront of the house stood toward the east, and the waters came down from under from the right side of the house, at the south side of the **altar.** |
| COMMENT | The details (east side, south side) seems to be specific and not symbolic. Ezekiel mentions one river whereas Zachariah 14:8 mentions two, however, both have a single source. Zachariah's river flows in two directions whereas Ezekiel's river just flows east. |
| 2 | Then brought he me out of the way of the gate northward, and led me about the way without unto the utter gate by the way that looketh eastward; and, behold, there ran out waters on the right side. |
| COMMENT | Water was flowing from an unexpected source to an unexpected destination. |
| 3 | And when the man that had the line in his hand went forth eastward, he measured **a thousand cubits**, and he brought me through the waters; the waters were to the ankles. |

| COMMENT | A cubit is about 18 inches. A 1000 cubits is 1500 feet or five football fields. The height of an ankle is about 6 inches. This is where the saying "you've got a lot to learn. You've just got your feet wet," originated. |
|---|---|
| 4 | Again he measured **a thousand**, and brought me through the waters; the waters were to the knees. Again he measured **a thousand**, and brought me through; the waters were to the loins. |
| COMMENT | 1500 + 1500 = 3000 feet. A loin is the hip or about 3 feet. |
| 5 | Afterward he measured **a thousand**; and it was a river that I could not pass over: for the waters were risen, waters to swim in, a river that could not be passed over. |
| COMMENT | Another 1500 feet. Total now is 4500 feet. There is 5,280 feet per mile. They have gone 4500/5280 = 85% of a mile and the water is over Ezekiel's head or, about 6 feet. It will flow through the Kidron Valley that is normally dry in the summer but, not now. Zechariah 14:8 says "in summer and winter shall it be." |
| 6 - 7 | And he said unto me, Son of man, hast thou seen this? Then he brought me, and caused me to return to the brink of the river.<br><br>Now when I had returned, behold, at the bank of the river were very many trees on the one side and on the other. |
| COMMENT | The water has grown trees on both banks of the river. |
| 8 | Then said he unto me, These waters issue out toward the east country, and go down into the desert, and go into the sea: which being brought forth into the sea, **the waters shall be healed.** |

| | |
|---|---|
| COMMENT | The "waters" is the Dead Sea. "Healed" means purified. Jerusalem is 2500 feet above sea level. The Dead Sea is at a −1400 feet. therefore, to go from Jerusalem to the Dead Sea is 2500 + 1400 = 3900 foot descent in 70 miles. This is about 3900/70 = 55 feet per mile or, one third of a football field. Try to picture one mile distance from your home and a stream falling one third of a football field in that distance. You do not have a stream. You have a torrent of water. It will hit the Dead Sea like it was a Niagara Falls.<br><br>The deepest valley rift in the world is the Arabah in the Holy Land. The waters of the river will flow east through Arabah into the Dead Sea." Arabah is an area south of the Dead Sea basin between Jordan and Israel. It covers the entire length of the Jordan Rift Valley. It is the "l" line in the above chart. What is a "rift." It is comparable to a valley except it is form by the separation of the earths tectronic plates. |
| 9 | 9And it shall come to pass, that everything that liveth, which moveth, whithersoever the rivers shall come, shall live: and there shall be a very great multitude of fish, because these waters shall come thither: **for they shall be healed**; and everything shall live whither the river cometh. |
| COMMENT | Whatsoever the waters touches is healed, including the Dead Sea. There is also an obvious but, possibly overlooked point here: God cares about the environment and promises to restore and heal it. Despite the many who worship the creation instead of the Creator, God Himself cares about His creation. His salvation and work of redemption extends to the environment. We are landlords of the Lord's land. |
| 10 | 10 And it shall come to pass, that the fishers shall stand upon it from Engedi even unto Eneglaim; they shall be a place to spread forth nets; their fish shall be according to their kinds, as the fish of the great sea, exceeding many. |

| | |
|---|---|
| COMMENT | Fishermen will spread their nets from En-Gedi ("fountain of a kid"), to En-Eglaim ("spring of the two calves"), both located on the western shore of the Dead Sea. The Dead Sea is about 31 miles long by 9 miles wide. That is a lot of fishing space. 31 miles is 163,630 feet. If we space the fisherman 100 feet apart, we would have 1,636 fisherman just on the west shore. The question may be asked, "If scripture is talking about the spread of Christianity, why are two cities mentioned with hundreds of fishermen? |
| 11 | 11 But the miry places thereof and the marshes thereof **shall not be healed**; they shall be given to salt. |
| COMMENT | At the southern end of the sea, Israel's Dead Sea Works and Jordan's Arab Potash Company evaporates the mineral-rich water to extract potash and magnesium. "It's the only place where Israel, Jordan and the Palestinian Authority are publicly working together on a project because they all need drinking water. Could this be God's plan to unite them? |
| 12 | 12 And by the river upon the bank thereof, on this side and on that side, shall grow all trees for meat, whose leaf shall not fade, neither shall the fruit thereof be consumed: it shall bring forth new fruit according to his months, because their waters they issued **out of the sanctuary**: and the fruit thereof shall be for **meat,** and the leaf thereof for **medicine.** |
| COMMENT | Revelation 22:1-2<br><br>1 And he shewed me **a pure river of water of life, clear as crystal, proceeding out of the throne of God and of the Lamb.**<br><br>2 In the midst of the street of it, and on either side of the river, *was there* the tree of life, **which bare twelve *manner of* fruits,** *and* yielded her fruit every month: and **the leaves of the tree *were* for the healing of the nations.**<br><br>This is not symbolic. It is real. How could Ezekiel know what the apostle John wrote hundreds of years later in Revelation? |

| GENERAL COMMENT | Those that adopt the spiritual interpretation of these verses do not include verses 8 and 9. Both verses say "these waters shall be healed." What waters? The Dead Sea is no longer dead. God has cured it. Verse 10 says fishermen will fish from Engedi to Eneglaim. Why mention fisherman? God is saying the sea is healed and produces edible food. |
| --- | --- |

There are current efforts to heal the Dead Sea. Obviously, Jordan, Israel and the Palestinians don't want to wait for Ezekiel's vision to become reality. They have jointly approached The World Bank for help.

Israel is considering two water-power projects. One is the MED-SEA that will bring water from the Mediterranean to the Dead Sea and the other is called the RED=SEA bringing water from the Red Sea to the Dead Sea. Israel, Jordan and the Palestinian Authority signed a RED-SEA agreement to build a 140-mile canal from the Red Sea to the Dead Sea.

If you consider all three at once, you have the Med-Red-Dead project. They plan to install desalination plants to change salt water to drinking water. The sea is dropping 1.2 meters (3 ½ feet) per year. It has lost 1/3 of its surface area in the last 100 years. I Have seen desalination plants when I lived in Saudi Arabia and they are massive. They extend for miles.

The Jordan River once fed the Dead Sea with 1.3 billion cubic meters of fresh water per year, but that has shriveled to less than 100 million cubic meters due to tapping the Jordan River for agriculture purposes and drinking water.

At the southern end of the sea, Israel's Dead Sea Works and Jordan's Arab Potash Company exacerbate the problem by evaporating the mineral-rich water to extract potash and magnesium. "It's the only place where Israel, Jordan and the Palestinian Authority are publicly working on a project together," But Gidon Bromberg, Israeli director of FoEME (Friends of the Earth Middle East), is not impressed. The FoEME is an environmental program. He says the potash companies could switch to extracting minerals by forcing Dead Sea water through membranes under high pressure. That would take more money and energy, but it would cause significantly less water to evaporate.

# OTHER INTERESTING EVENTS

## AMANTHA SIEGEL

Is the Dead Sea beginning to heal? She visits the Dead Sea each year and has publically produced a video showing fish swimming and green plants.

## BEN GURION UNIVERSITY AT NEGEV

In 2011 researchers from the university sent divers to the floor of the sea and discovered huge craters measuring 15 meters across and 20 meters deep that were gushing fresh water. This brings to mind what Job said about "springs of the sea" and Genesis said about "fountains of the great deep." Job 38:16. A meter is roughly 3 feet after "fresh water."

> 16 Hast thou entered into the **springs of the sea**? or hast thou walked in the search of the depth?

Genesis 7:11.

11 In the six hundredth year of Noah's life, in the second month, the seventeenth day of the month, the same day were all **the fountains of the great deep** broken up, and the windows of heaven were opened.

This happened during the Noah flood. Water came from two directions. It came down as 150 days of rain. It came up when the fountains of the deep broke open. I believe that the waters that first lifted the ark were from the fountains of the great deep.

Astonishing news! 2011. "Israel's Largest Underground Water Source Discovered near Jerusalem International Convention Center." The center is near the Temple mount. Could this be the source of water that flows from the temple?

Of all the major ancient cities, Israel is the only one without a river. That will change as shown in Appendix 8. The water source was found by Israel Railways while working on a high speed Jerusalem to Tel Aviv train line. They were digging an 80 foot shaft and found it at 75 feet, just 5 foot from stopping. Scholars from the Cave Research Unit of the Hebrew University's Department of Geography, explored the cave. The cave is 2 meters wide (about 6 feet) and 24 meters (about 80 feet) high.

The cave developed as water seeped in from the surface and dissolved the limestone. It is called a karstic cave, named after the region in Slovenia where the phenomenon was first documented. Water was flowing from northwest to the southeast. The cave is estimated to be about 200 meters long. A canyon at the end has a series of waterfalls. This proves that underground streams are common and extends all along Israel's central mountain range.

Ezekiel 47:1-12 may be interpreted symbolically and be used as fodder for sermons. However, literal interpretations are still alive and well. The existing faults and underground water sources lend creditability to the literal interpretation of Ezekiel chapter 47 as do the comments on fishing.

It is understandable that Jordan, Israel and the Palestinians want to produce clean water by building the RED SEA and MED-SEA projects to desalinate the water and flow it into the Dead Sea to heal/purify it. They want it done yesterday. What is not understandable is why Israel is not relying on God to fulfill Ezekiel's RIDS (Resurrect Inert Dead Sea). RIDS is the author's term. Webster defines inert as "not having the power to move itself" or "lacking chemical reaction." God can overcome inertness through our prayers and belief. When we pray, the answer to prayer is yes, no, wait (not now). God is in control. Is Israel relying on funding rather than faith?

Another question may be posed. What if the new temple is not on the Temple Mount?

Currently, Israel is considering building the third temple on the Temple Mount which would be contested by rival religions. The Temple Mount was the site of the first and second Jewish temples. It is most importance to Jews and Moslems. It can be entered through 11 gates, 10 for Muslims and one for non-Muslims. Jewish tradition maintains it is here that a third and final temple will be built.

Sunni Muslims consider it as the third holiest site were Muhammad ascended to heaven. Umayyad, a Muslim, built the Dome of the Rock and the al-Aqsa Mosque on the site in 692. The Muslims have managed the site under a Waqf which is an Islamic religious trust that is managed by Jordan. Israel allowed the waqf to remain in existence after they won the 6 day war in 1967. Muslims have warned Israel not to build the temple there or there would be war.

Archaeologist Vendyl Jones proposed Gilgal would be the best location. It is near Jericho and the Jordan River. This is where Israel anointed their kings. Water could easily flow south to the Dead Sea. A slight shift in the Jordan Rift fault would hasten the process.

It has been reported that during the presidency of USA President Donald Thrump, that he and Vladimir Putin, President of Russia, were involved in planning and funding the building of the temple in Jerusalem. This could possibly be a doable do because the Muslims might think twice about engaging the worlds two top powers in war?

# APPENDIX 7

# THE LAMB IS MARRIED

Part of the trinity being married is not a new concept. In the Old Testament God claimed to be the spouse of Israel. Jeremiah 3:14, Hosea 2:16.

> **14** Turn, O backsliding children, saith the LORD; for **I am married unto you**: and I will take you one of a city, and two of a family, and I will bring you to Zion:

> **16** And it shall be at that day, saith the LORD, *that* **thou shalt call me Ishi; and shalt call me no more Baali.**

"Ishi" in the Hebrew means "My husband" and "Baali" means "My master."

Hosea 2:19-20.

19 And I will **betroth** thee unto me forever; yea, I will **betroth** thee unto me in righteousness, and in judgment, and in loving kindness, and in mercies.

20 I will even **betroth** thee unto me in faithfulness: and thou shalt know the LORD.

Isaiah 54:5

5 For **thy Maker** *is* **thine husband**; the LORD of hosts *is* his name; and thy Redeemer the Holy One of Israel; The God of the whole earth shall he be called.

We can read where God considered his relationship to Israel as one of marriage. God married a nation. Jesus is going to marry a church in Revelation 19:7

7 Let us be glad and rejoice, and give honour to him: **for the marriage of the Lamb is come**, and his wife hath made herself ready.

What is meant by "lamb"? In the Old Testament they would sacrifice animals that were "without spot or blemish." Lambs were one of them. In the New Testament Jesus is the Christian's lamb. He was sacrificed for our sins. John the Baptist referred to him as the Lamb of God. John 1:29.

29 The next day John seeth Jesus coming unto him, and saith, **Behold the Lamb of God**, which taketh away the sin of the world.

We now know that the "lamb" is Jesus and Revelation 21:9-10 tells us his bride is "the holy Jerusalem." Revelation 21:9-10.

> **9** And there came unto me one of the seven angels which had the seven vials full of the seven last plagues, and talked with me, saying, Come hither, **I will shew thee the bride, the Lamb's wife.**

> **10** And he carried me away in the spirit to a great and high mountain, and shewed me **that great city, the holy Jerusalem,** descending out of heaven from God,

There will be a celebration. Revelation 19:9.

> **9** And he saith unto me, Write, Blessed *are* they which are called unto the marriage supper of the Lamb. And he saith unto me, These are the true sayings of God.

Who are the "blessed"? Those whose names are written in The Book of Life.

God had Jesus send out RSVPs (Respondez sil vous plait) inviting all of the truly saved to the super. Scholars mostly agree that the marriage is in heaven and the supper is on earth during the millennium. Revelation 20:15 talks about those that are truly saved.

> 15 And whosoever was not found written in the book of life was cast into the lake of fire.

> What is the book of life? Following are some scriptures addressing it. Phil. 4:3, Rev 3:5, Rev 13;8, Rev 20:12.

> 4:3 And I intreat thee also, true yokefellow, help those women which laboured with me in the

gospel, with Clement also, and with other my fellow labourers, whose names are in the **book of life**.

3:5 He that overcometh, the same shall be clothed in white raiment; and I will not blot out his name out of the **book of life**, but I will confess his name before my Father, and before his angels.

13:8 And all that dwell upon the earth shall worship him, whose names are not written in the **book of life** of the Lamb slain from the foundation of the world.

20:12 And I saw the dead, small and great, stand before God; and the books were opened: and another book was opened, which is the **book of life**: and the dead were judged out of those things which were written in the books, according to their works.

How do you get your name in the book? Accept Jesus as your savior. There are very few, if any, in the USA that have not heard the message of salvation. Some reject it and some postpone it. Both are saying no to Jesus and are not named in The Book of Life. This takes place at the Great White Throne judgment. It will be quick. If your name is not in the book, you and Satan's devils are headed to an eternity in hell. If you name is in the book (Christians) you will live an eternity in heaven. That's good information but, how do I get my name in the Book of Life? Pray;

1 – Asking God to forgive you of your sins.
2 – Accepting Jesus as your savior.
3 – Asking God to walk with you in the Christian life.
4 – Amen.

Find a church that preaches Jesus and Him crucified.
Get baptized.
Study and attend church.
Grow in the faith.

Congratulations! You are in The Book of Life. You will not attend the White Throne Judgment. I hope you will enjoy Jesus wedding supper.

# APPENDIX 8

# JESUS SPLITS A MOUNTAIN, ISRAEL GETS A SEAPORT, THE DEAD SEA IS HEALED

The return of our Lord has been discussed by many scholars. Scriptures say He will return to the same spot where He ascended. He has a round trip ticket to heaven and back. Only God knows when his return flight will take off. His first flight took off on The Mount of Olives and His return landing will be the same place. He is flying first class. Some have proposed that He will return to Bethany and not the Mount of Olives. Luke 24:50-51.

> **50** And **he led them out as far as to Bethany**, and he lifted up his hands, and blessed them.
>
> **51** And it came to pass, while he blessed them, **he was parted from them, and carried up into heaven.**

A glance at the map shows that Bethany is on the slope of the Mount of Olives. Acts 1:9-12 gives us more information.

> **9** And when he had spoken these things, while they beheld, **he was taken up;** and a cloud received him out of their sight.

> **10** And while they looked stedfastly toward heaven as he went up, behold, two men stood by them in white apparel;

> **11** Which also said, Ye men of Galilee, why stand ye gazing up into heaven? this same Jesus, which is taken up from you into heaven, shall so come in **like manner** as ye have seen him go into heaven.

> **12** Then returned they unto Jerusalem from the mount called Olivet, which is from Jerusalem a sabbath day's journey.

Verse 12 says they returned from The Mount of Olives to Jerusalem. Luke was just more specific when he mentioned Bethany that was located on the Mount of Olives. A Sabbath day's journey was ½ mile and was created when the Jews wandered in the desert.

Why did Jesus choose The Mount of Olives? It was accessible to Jerusalem. Some facts about it are,

1 - It is named for the <u>olive groves</u> that once covered its slopes.

2 - The southern part of the Mount was the Silwan necropolis which is the old Judean kingdom.

3 – It has been a <u>Jewish cemetery</u> for over 3,000 years with 150,000 graves. It would be vacant at night. Jesus may have slept in it?

4 – Jesus would ascend from it and return to it.

5- Jesus spent time on the mount, teaching and prophesying to his disciples, including the <u>Olivet discourse,</u>

6 – Gethsemane lies at the foot of the Mount of Olives. After their last super Jesus and his disciples went there. This is where Jesus was arrested and the disciples all fled.

Lets turn our attention to the splitting of the mountain. Matthew 27:50-51.

> **50** Jesus, when he had cried again with a loud voice, yielded up the ghost.

> **51** And, behold, the veil of the temple was rent in twain from the top to the bottom; and **the earth did quake, and the rocks rent;**

The Lord's death caused an earthquake. His return will cause another one that splits The Mount of Olives. Although we do not hear much on the news about earthquakes in the Holy Land, there has been quite a few. In this year (2021) alone there has been 5 earthquakes near Jerusalem.

What is the power of an earthquake? In 1811the Mississippi Valley quake reverse the flow of the river. The series of quakes measured 8.4, 8.6, 8.8. We must remember that when a quake grows from one whole number to another (i.e., 5 to 6) it means that 6 is 10 times stronger than a 5, 7 is ten times larger than a 6 and etc. This was the strongest earthquake in the USA. Note that it was Mississippi and not California.

Years ago, The Intercontinental Hotel was building The Seven Arches Hotel atop The mount of Olives when they discovered a fault line beneath it. Construction stopped. Our Lord has plans to use that fault when He returns. Zechariah 14:4-5.

> **4** And his feet shall stand in that day upon **the mount of Olives**, which *is* before Jerusalem on the east, and **the mount of Olives shall cleave in the midst thereof toward the east and toward the west,** *and there shall be* **a very great valley; and half of the mountain shall remove toward the north, and half of it toward the south.**

> **5** And **ye shall flee** *to* **the valley of the mountains;** for the valley of the mountains shall reach unto Azal: yea, ye shall flee, like as ye fled from before the earthquake in the days of Uzziah king of Judah: and the LORD my God shall come, *and* all the saints with thee.

This brings to mind Matthew 17:20.

> **20** And Jesus said unto them, Because of your unbelief: for verily I say unto you, **If ye have faith as a grain of mustard seed, ye shall say unto this mountain, Remove hence to yonder place; and it shall remove;** and nothing shall be impossible unto you.

Jesus moved a mountain.

| NORTH | Mt Scopus |
|--------|-------------------|
| VALLEY | EAST TO WEST |
| SOUTH | Mt of Corruption |

The mountain was split from east to west that created a valley. The peak to the north is Mount Scopus at 2,710 feet. The peak to the south is Mount of Corruption at 2,684 feet. The difference in heights is just 26 feet (2710 – 2684 = 26) which is ideal for dividing (splitting) the two peaks.

Verse 5 gives the Jews an avenue of escape from their enemies. Azal is east of the Mount of Olives at Wadi Yasul, a tributary of the Kidron which is dry in the summer and wet in the winter. It flows through the 20 mile valley of Jehoshaphat and drops 3,912 feet and enters the Jordon River. The Kidron Valley is also called the Valley of the Kings or the Garden of the Kings. Ez 14:8.

> 8 And it shall be in that day, that living waters shall go out from Jerusalem; **half of them toward the former sea,** and **half of them toward the hinder sea:** in summer and in winter shall it be.

What is happening? We have a spring between two halves of a split mountain. Half of it flows to the former sea (Mediterreanean) and half towards the hinder sea (Dead Sea). It is Israel's first seaport. Because it is spring fed, ships coming to the port from either sea will be travelling upstream against the current.

## FINAL COMMENTS

Because Jesus has "landed" on the Mount of Olives, we know this occurred at His return to set up His kingdom. The Great Tribulation has ended and the millennium has begun. Satan is bound for 1,000 years. This is His third visit to earth. Two involved landings and one was a fly-by. The landings were His birth and His return after the Great Tribulation. The fly by was the rapture. When Christ resurrects the saved church, He doesn't land. Instead, the saved are drawn up to meet Him in the air. It is a fly-by.

Many believe the return of Jesus will initiate the rapture then, the tribulation. The sequence of events are debated amongst scholars. Does it really matter? Books have been written that detail the sequence of events in the Book of Revelation as though each author is an authority. I am not one of those. What matters is that your resurrection destination is heaven and not hell. Both are eternal. Don't worry about the events relative to your trip. God will handled all travel arrangements.

Appendix 6 talked about waters flowing from the temple to the Dead Sea and healing the sea. This would not be true if we accepted the sysmbolic interpretation. However, when we read this appendix, we see where the Dead Sea is getting plenty of fresh (spring) water that will heal it. Fishing will be great. Ez 47:10.

> 10And it shall come to pass, that the fishers shall stand upon it from Engedi even unto Eneglaim; they shall be a place to spread forth nets; their fish shall be according to their kinds, as the fish of the great sea, exceeding many.

# APPENDIX 9

# WHEN WILL CHRIST RETURN?

Why would God not want to tell us? The cleanest you will find some homes is when they are expecting company. If we knew that Christ was coming back next Thursday, we would all be good little girls and boys. We would be asking all of our neighbors If they were Christians. Some may even write large checks to foreign missions. What were the conditions of the people when the Noah flood occurred? Matthew 24:38-39.

> 38 For as in the days that were before the flood they were eating and drinking, marrying and giving in marriage, until the day that Noe entered into the ark,
>
> 39 **And knew not until the flood came, and took them all away; so shall also the coming of the Son of man be.**

God wants to find us in our real environment and not a fake one. Another reason He has not told us a date for the return of Jesus is

He expects us to watch with anticipation. We know He is returning but, not knowing the exact date, means we need to "be on our toes." I remember when WWII ended and numerous members of my family were to be discharged and headed home. I was the youngest of 13 children. They showed up unexpected, one at a time. We did not know who was coming next or when. Jesus wanted us to have a sense of urgency about His return i.e., it could happen anytime, perhaps before you finish reading this sentence? Following are some verses that illustrate what is meant by urgency.

| BOOK | VERSE | SCRIPTURE |
|---|---|---|
| Matthew | 3:1-2 | **1** In those days came John the Baptist, preaching in the wilderness of Judaea, <br><br> **2** And saying, Repent ye: for the kingdom of heaven is **at hand.** |
| Matthew | 10:6-7 | **6** But go rather to the lost sheep of the house of Israel. <br><br> **7** And as ye go, preach, saying, The kingdom of heaven is **at hand.** |
| Matthew | 10:21-23 | **23** But when they persecute you in this city, flee ye into another: for verily I say unto you, **Ye shall not have gone over the cities of Israel, till the Son of man be come.** |
| Matthew | 16:27-28 | **27** For **the Son of man** shall come in the glory of his Father with his angels; and then he shall reward every man according to his works. <br><br> **28** Verily I say unto you, **There be some standing here, which shall not taste of death, till they see the Son of man coming in his kingdom.** |
| Matthew | 24:34 | **34 Verily I say unto you, This generation shall not pass, till all these things be fulfilled.** |

| Mark | 1:14-15 | 14 Now after that John was put in prison, Jesus came into Galilee, preaching the gospel of the kingdom of God,<br><br>15 And saying, The time is fulfilled, and **the kingdom of God is at hand**: repent ye, and believe the gospel. |
| --- | --- | --- |
| Philippians | 4:5 | 5 Let your moderation be known unto all men. The Lord *is* **at hand.** |
| James | 5:8-9 | 8 Be ye also patient; stablish your hearts: for the coming of **the Lord draweth nigh.**<br><br>9 Grudge not one against another, brethren, lest ye be condemned: behold, **the judge standeth before the door.** |
| 1 Peter | 4:7,17 | 7 But the end of all things **is at hand**: be ye therefore sober, and watch unto prayer.<br><br>17 For **the time** *is come* **that judgment must begin** at the house of God: and if *it* first *begin* at us, what shall the end *be* of them that obey not the gospel of God? |
| Revelation | 1:3 | 3 Blessed *is* he that readeth, and they that hear the words of this prophecy, and keep those things which are written therein: **for the time** *is* **at hand.** |
| Revelation | 22:20-21 | 20 He which testifieth these things saith, **Surely I come quickly.** Amen. Even so, come, Lord Jesus.<br><br>21 The grace of our Lord Jesus Christ *be* with you all. Amen. |

We need to learn some terminology before analyzing the above table. The "Son of man" designates Christ as mankind and the last Adam. "Son of God" designates Christ as the highest of God's creatures. The "son of God" is not used in the table but the "son of man is used twice i.e., Matthew 10:21-23, 16:27-28 refers to His resurrection and ascension.

Matthew 24:34 refers to fulfillment of Old Testament prophecies. There are 6 entries in the above table that says the second coming of Christ "is at hand." James 5:8-9 says "it draweth nigh." The authors are writing this because that is what they were taught. Notice that Matthew led the books with 5 warnings. Matthew was writing to the Jews and saying "make up your minds, time is running short."

In the last book of the bible (Revelation) in the last chapter and just before the last verse of the bible, Jesus speaks. Revelation 22:20. "Surely I come quickly." You will notice that Matthew 16:27-28, 24:34 in the above table leads one to believe those listening to Jesus would see His return. How would Jesus know when He would return if only God knew the date? Scholars claim these passages were fulfilled with the Transfiguration.

Notice the words "some standing here." Only Jesus inner circle (James, John and Peter) witnessed the transfiguration.

Jesus has been waiting on marching orders from God for thousands of years. Why?

1 - 2 Peter 3:9.

> 9 The Lord is not slack concerning his promise, as some men count slackness; but is longsuffering to us-ward, **not willing that any should perish,** but that all should come to repentance.

Have you ever been trying to accomplish something and had to give it one last try such as playing a card game of solitaire or casting a lure while fishing. "Just one more time!" Could God be doing the same thing? Missionaries are active in the field and God may not want to stop it? Some claim that the New Testament is being translated into

2700 languages in167 countries. Not only are people being saved but Christians are earning rewards and crowns.

2 – God is omnipresent, He can see into the future. Perhaps He is looking at a large group becoming Christians 25 years from now? It would be difficult for Him to stop it by initiating the return of Jesus.

3 – The actors have not yet been casted. Let's go back to the end of the Old Testament. The people could have asked, "where is the Messiah God promised?" A hundred years when by and no Messiah. Then another hundred, then another hundred, etc.. Alexander the Great conquered us and no Messiah. Rome conquered us and no Messiah. When will the Messiah appear? What is happening today happened to the Jews at the end of the Old Testament. Why did Jesus arrive 400 years after the close of the Old Testament? One answer is that the actors were not yet cast. What actors? John the Baptist, Mary and Joseph, Herod, Pilate, Judas, Paul, the apostles, etc.. We are not talking about a person but, rather a group of people.

When you are putting on a stage show, you need a cast of actors, not just a star. William Shakespeare compare life to a stage and all of us as actors in his pastora; comedy "As you like it,." When he said "all the world's a stage and all the men and women merely players."

4 – Another reason was that prophecy addressed the cross which was a Roman form of execution. Because Israel was occupied by the Romans the Jews were not allowed to use their own methods of capital punishment. They had to find Jesus guilty of treason in order for Rome to kill him. He claimed to be King of the Jews. That did it!

Matthew 24:7 says there will be famines, pestilences and earthquakes. These are problems stemming from natural resources. One source is outer space. Following is a list of outer space objects that may be involved.

## SPACE OBJECTS

| OBJECT | DEFINITION |
|---|---|
| METEOR | A shooting star. A meteor that burns up in the sky. |
| METEORITE | A meteor that hits the earth. |
| COMET | An active object composed of dirt and ice that has a gaseous tail. |
| ASTEROID | An active body composed of rock, carbon or metal. |
| PLANETOID | A large asteroid. |
| NEO | Near Earth Object |

Here is what researchers have to say. NASA's Ames Research Centre in California. Future impacts will happen. NASA is tracking 1,397 of them.

Within the next 500 years more than 1,000 objects the size of a football field will hit the earth. Some impacts could be greater than the atomic bombs dropped on Japan in World War II. Objects of .6 miles in diameter could hit the earth killing millions.

## EXAMPLES OF RECORDED EVENTS
Contribution; Wikipedia, Meteors

| YEAR | SIZE | ACTIVITY |
|---|---|---|
| Paleogene +Period | The Chicxulub Crater in the Yucatan Peninsula South America is 180km (110 miles) in diameter and 20km (12 miles) in depth. The NEO was about 60 miles in diameter (planetoid) and is thought to have made the dinosaurs extinct. The author audited the NASA Ames Research Lab that is studying the subject. | |
| 1908 | Not stated | 2000 km square (1.5 square miles) of forest burned in Siberia |
| 1972 | 1000 Ton | Flew over the Grand Tetons National Park in Wyoming |
| 1992 | 12.4 KG (27 lbs) | Seen over Peekskill NY |

| 19 Jan 1993 | 145 kilotons of energy | Exploded over Lugo Italy |
|---|---|---|
| 1995-1992 | 136 airbursts greater than 1 kiloton | Stated by the Department of Energy-could be 10 times greater because data was not recorded for all of earth. |
| 1994 | P/Shoemaker-Levy 9 comet | The Hubble telescope recorded the comet impacting Jupiter. Temperatures rose to 20,000 degrees and shot a fireball thousands of miles into space. |
| 15 Feb 2013 | 30 kilo tons TNT | Chelyabinsk meteor passed over Russia at 42,900 miles per hour and exploded in the air at an elevation of 18 miles, injuring 1500 people. 30 kilo tons of TNT is about 25 time greater than the bombs dropped on Japan in WWII |
| 2014 | 1000 asteroids | Being tracked by NASA |
| December 2016 | NEO asteroid 2003 SD220 | The closest asteroid to earth being tracked by NASA. The closest approach in 400 years. |

October 1, 2014 - Russia and the USA are working on plans to mitigate meteor impacts. They are retaining nuclear war heads to be deployed should asteroids approach earth. The problem may be that they could create fragments that still hit earth.

Based on chapters 6 and 8 of The Revelation, and what we know about asteroids, it is very probable that God could use his own creation to destroy what he created. He created the outer space bodies and could use them as his tools to accomplish what John has written. He used what he created during the Noah flood to destroy all but eight people and he could do it again. Revelation 8:10-11.

> **10** And the third angel sounded, and **there fell a great star from heaven, burning as it were a lamp**, and it fell upon the third part of the rivers, and upon the fountains of waters;

> **11** And **the name of the star is called Wormwood:** and the third part of the waters became wormwood; and many men died of the waters, because they were made bitter.

Wormwood in the Greek is "laanah" which means "undrinkable" and is used to express bitterness. Gall is made from it. That is what they tried to give Jesus on the cross when he said "I thirst" John 19;28. "Mountain size" could extinguish all life. God has used "brimstone and fire" before and will use it again. Could these be objects from outer space?

A meteorite travels through space (a vacuum) at tens of thousands miles per hour. When it enters the earth's atmosphere its gas is compressed and it heats to 3000 degrees F. That is hot! Genesis 19:24.

> **24** Then the LORD **rained upon Sodom and upon Gomorrah brimstone and fire** from the LORD **out of heaven;**

Notice that it came from heaven and not some sulphur pit. Revelation 20:8-9, 21.

> **8** And shall go out to deceive the nations which are in the four quarters of the earth, **Gog and Magog**, to gather them together to battle: the number of whom *is* as the sand of the sea.

> **9** And they went up on the breadth of the earth, and compassed the camp of the saints about, and the beloved city: and **fire came down from God out of heaven**, and devoured them.

21 And there fell upon men a **great hail out of heaven**, every stone **about the weight of a talent:** and men blasphemed God because of the plague of the hail; for the plague thereof was exceeding great.

Notice in verse 9 that fire came "came down from God" and verse 21talks about "great hail out of heaven." Most people tend to think about a nuclear war but, God can use parts of His own creation to accomplish His purposes if He so chooses.

Notice that everything is coming down from heaven and not up. He used fire and brimstone in Genesis and could use it again in Revelation. These could very well be meteorite showers. A talent (verse 21) is about 93 pounds. That is a huge hot (30,000F) stone. As it falls from the sky, it would burst through a roof and keep falling until it hit solid concrete.

Jews have established criteria for the coming of their Mashiach. Contribution; Wikipedia, Mashiach, the Messiah.

| |
|---|
| 1- When Israel repents for one day. |
| 2-When Israel correctly observes one Shabbat. |
| 3-When Israel correctly observes two Shabbats in a row. |
| 4- When a generation is totally innocent or totally guilty. |
| 5- When a generation loses hope. |
| 6- When a generation of children disrespects their parents and elders. |
| RESPONSE |
| 1 – Repentance is not by the day. It is forever. |
| 2 & 3- These contradict one another. You don't observe God's law once or twice, you continually observe it. |
| 4- How does one determine "totally? |
| 5, 6 - Generation for the Hebrews is 40 years. |

God will determine the second coming of Jesus, not man.
Mark 13:32.

32 But of that day and that hour knoweth no man, no, not the angels
which are in heaven, neither the Son, but the Father.

NOTE: We trust that the Jews have informed God when Christ will return so He can meet their schedule? Look at item #2 (observe one Sabbath
correctly). If that is all it would take to have the Mashiach return, why
haven't they done it? What is so difficult about having one good Saturday?

We need to address the title of Mashiach. It means Messiah. The
Jews stopped referring to the Messiah and started using Mashiach
because the gentiles were using Messiah. Jews are forbidden to read
Is 52:13-53:12 (suffering servant chapters) because it is convincing
evidence that Jesus is the Messiah and they would have to admit it.

Some people have tried to set dates for the return of Jesus. Jews
determine the date of the end time as the year 2239 per their Olam
Ha-Ba. This is the Jewish "Messianic Age" (The World to Come).
The world will recognize the Jewish God as the only God and their
religion as the only true religion. Olam Ha-Ba is compared to Olam
ha-the (the world of today). One question that has always plagued
the Jews is "When will the Mashiach come?" Many have tried to put
a date on future events, including the Jews. The word Messiah" is
not in the Talmud although the Talmud does mention the end times.

The Jewish Talmud sets a date for the end time. It is called Olam
Ba Ha. They set each of the six creation days equivalent to 1,000
years. God created the universe in 6 days thus, the end times will be
in 6000 years. They say the creation took place in the year 3761BC
and their current year as of 2019AD is the year 5780. Contribution;
Wikipedia Olam HaBa value in Gem Gematir Calculator.

| |
|---|
| 5780 their current year (2019) |
| -2019 |
| 3761 – the world was created. |
| 6000 the End Times begin |
| -5780 their current year (2019) |
| 220 years to end times |
| 2019 now |
| +220 End Times begin = 2239 |

According to the Jews the End Times begin in the year 2239. 2239 – 2019 = 220 years to go! That may be true but, Billy Graham said years ago that all of the signs of the second coming have been fulfilled.

Jesus gave us signs to look for relative to His return during the Olivet Discourse when He was talking to His inner circle which were two sets of brothers i.e., James and John and Peter and Andrew. Matthew 24, 25, Mark 13, Luke 21. Although we don't know the exact date of His return, He gave us some signs that indicates His return is near.

1 – Many will come in His name. Matthew 24:4-5. See #5 and #10 below.

2 – There will be wars and rumors of wars. Matthew 24:6-7.

There has been 27 incidents where Jerusalem was either captured, possessed, or defeated. Events in recent years have involved the Golan Heights, Yom Kippur war and Lebanon. Christ said we are to be aware when Israel is surrounded by armies. It is easy for a country to be surrounded with the aerial capability of many countries. Any country can be surrounded by any other country using missiles.

3 – There will be natural disasters and famines. Matthew 24:7

Following is a partial list of disasters. In most cases, famine follows the disaster. Contribution; Wikipedia, List of natural disasters by death toll. Ten deadliest disasters by highest estimated death ntoll excluding epidemics and famines.

| YEAR | COUNTRY | EVENT | DEATHS |
|------|---------|-------|--------|
| 526 | Antioch, Syria | Earthquake | 250,000 |
| 1138 | Aleppo, Syria | Earthquake | 230,000 |
| 1556 | Shaanxi China | Earthquake | 830,000 |
| 1839 | Coringa, Bengal | Cyclone | 300,000 |
| 1887 | Yellow River, China | Flood | 900,000 |
| 1918 | Global pandemic | Flu virus | 30 to 50M, USA= 675,000 |
| 1920 | Haiyuan, China | Earthquake | 273,400 |
| 1970 | Bhola, China | Cyclone | 500,000 |
| 1976 | Tangshan, China | Earthquake | 240,000 |
| 2020 | World wide | Covid 19 virus | 3,381,269 |
| SUM | | | 35,046,269 |
| NOTE | At the time of this writing, COVID has generated a new virus that has killed millions and is being fought world-wide. | | |

Although some countries have received more blessings from God than others, the USA heads the list. We have been involved in over 100 government legislated conflicts but, other than the revolutionary war and the French and Indian wars, no other country has invaded our shore. We have fought wars in foreign countries. The gospel has been expounded throughout the USA. No one can claim ignorance of God's word. Yet, the USA has violated God's word as much, or more, than any other country. We know more of God's demands and are, therefore, more responsible. Other countries are guilty of sins as well. To that end, has God developed a global chastisement of all nations? Is it COVID19 (2019 is the year it was discovered)?

The yearly trends involved the spring, summer and fall. The summer rate was higher than the spring and the fall rate was 4 to 5 times higher than the summer rate. The fall death rates have been climbing each day for weeks. Many people did not adhere to wearing a mask, social distancing, and etc during the Thanksgiving holidays and the airlines were full of travelers. Deaths rates are expected to increase even more. To compound things even more, today is Christmas day and the gathering of family members plus nation-wide travel is expected to raise death rates even higher.

A new strand of the virus has emerged. One half of the USA has not been vaccinated and have a high rate of infection. My oldest daughter, her husband and daughter have the Covid virus. None have been vaccinated. They live in Mississippi which has the highest rate of infections. There are no available hospital beds in the entire state. Her husband died of the virus.

In recent days Los Angeles, California has 50,000 cases for two days in a row. The ICUs (Internal Care Units) are full. Refrigerated truck are picking up the bodies. They have no room to admit patients such as heart attack or car accidents. On the bright side, we have two new vaccines that have been in use for one week. Returning to the dark side, we have new, and more deadly, viruses (20AEU1) appearing in European countries but, predominately in England, Africa and Brazil. Is God punishing the globe but concentrating on the USA. The USA has about 19 million cases. The next highest country has about 10 million. The USA is being punished the most. One wonders where are the Christian preachers that should be addressing all of this? They preach a lot of "goody goody" sermons that people want to hear but, are shy about preaching God's wrath. We have slapped God in His face and He can slap back.

4 – The saints will be offended and turn against one another. Matthew 24:9-10. The world will be segregated into the saved and the unsaved (wheat and tares). The unsaved will rule. Same sex marriages, sodomy, abortion, Hollywood sex shows, and etc. will attract many. The state of Oregon has just announced (2021) the

legal sale of all drugs. Availability will entice many to try them. Churches will become more lenient. I know of a church that dismissed a homosexual preacher. He was hired by another church within one mile of the church that fired him. Would you attend it?

5 – There will be many false prophets. Matthew 24:11. The USA has an estimated 5,000 cults. That is an average of 100 cults per state. They attract, among others, High School and College students. In order to guard against the "isms," fathers need to be teaching their children. I just talked to a man today that is spending time with his daughter to learn the bible. He is the exception. I am age 85 and he is the only father I know that does it. Do you know of any? One might raise the question, "do the fathers know the bible enough to teach it"? If Christ is not part of the home, we make our children targets for alcoholism, drugs and the "isms."

6 – Because there will be so much evil, the love of the saints will diminish but, they that endure to the end shall be saved. Matthew 24:12-13. We will refer to them as postage stamp Christians. They will stick until delivered. Think about Sodom. God said He would spare the city if they could find 10 righteous people. Actually, that really means six because we can assume Lot, his wife and two daughters were righteous? Sodom is where the word sodomy comes from. Think about Noah. Genesis 5:6 says mankind's thoughts were "evil continually." Now think about the USA. If a majority thinks something is right, it becomes legal. This occurred with same sex marriage, sodomy, assisted suicide, abortion and etc. The government made them all legal which is just another way of saying they told God to take a walk. Since killing unborn babies was legalized in 1973 via the Roe-Wade Act, 1.7 million babies have been murdered by doctors who are suppose to save lives. This is a span of 48 years.

# THE ABORTION KILL RATE.

Contribution; Wikipedia, Total abortions since 1973. 62,502,904.

| By the year | By the month | By the day | By the hour |
|---|---|---|---|
| 1,588.555 – 1985 | 132,379 | 4412 | 183 |

Can you imagine a doctor returning home after a days work and sitting down to a super with his wife. She asks, "how many babies did we kill today dear?" "How many were girls and how many were boys?" "Was there any late term babies? Did we salvage any body parts for resale?" How much did we make selling them? The doctor responds with the information and both rejoice over their income for the day. After dinner they prepare to attend a mid-night service at their church. It is Christmas eve! What do you think God thinks? The USA just finished a presidential election in which the Democrats won. Democrats not only support abortion, they fund it. President Biden is a catholic and the churches stance on abortion is they are against it. How will the church and the President deal with it? We know what God thinks about abortion. Can this problem be solved by Biden confessing his sin and the priest forgives him? Is that the way God forgives?

The average American is bombarded with acts of sin stemming from Hollywood and TV to where many accept it as the norm. The government legalizes these sins under the guise that people have the right to choose. This year, Oregon was the first state to legalize sale of small amounts of cocaine, heroin, methamphetamine and other drugs. Advocates cite the success of Portugal when they did the same thing in 2001. They average 3 in 1,000,000 deaths. They are next to the lowest rate out of 30 European countries. Why not use the love of God? Jesus can cure an addiction.

7 – The Great Commission will be fulfilled. The gospel will be preached in all the world. The author donates to organizations who

are translating the scripture into local languages around the world. They expect to have all languages to be translated in the next ten years. The final sermon, in all languages, will be in accordance with Revelation 14:6-7. It will be preached to all of the world in all languages. Everyone will understand the message where they can make a choice.

8 – Daniel's Abomination of Desolation stands in the "holy place." The phrase abomination of desolation could refer to three events.

First is when the Greek King Antiochus IV replaced the Jewish sacrifices on the altar with a pig.

Second may be when Titus of Rome destroyed the temple in 70AD.

Third is futuristic.

Amillenist say this event has occurred whereas, premillenist say it has yet to occur.

9 – Matthew 24:16 – 22 describes the horror of the events to come and warns people to flee immediately without preparing to leave. It also mentions that the days will be shortened for the sake of the elect (Christians).

10 – Matthew 24:23-26. There will be false prophets.


## THOSE THAT HAVE CLAIMED MESSIAHSHIP
Contribution; Wikipedia, List of Messiah Claimants'

| CATEGORY | AMOUNT |
|----------|--------|
| Jewish | 15 |
| Christian | 24 |
| 18TH Century | 7 |

| 19th Century | 6 |
|---|---|
| 20th Century | 25 |
| 21st Century | 5 |
| TOTAL | 82 |

It is amazing that anyone would claim to be the messiah. One lady even claimed to be the sister of the virgin Mary. God knows it is a lie and can exact swift punishment. It can be viewed as spiritual suicide.

One of the most recent was Jim Jones who claimed to be the messiah of his church (The Peoples Temple) in Jonestown, Guyana South America. After murdering Congressman Leo Ryan and his team of four, he led 918 people in suicide then, shot himself, Just another fake messiah. Those trying to counterfeit Jesus are actually saying Jesus is real. One never counterfeits something false. Who would counterfeit a $75 bill?

Following is the Olivet Discourse where Jesus was talking to two sets of brothers; James and John and Peter and Andrew. What Jesus said is recorded in Matthew, Mark and Luke as shown next.

# THE OLIVET DISCOURSE

| MATTHEW 24 | MARK 13 | LUKE 21 |
|---|---|---|
| 1- And Jesus went out, and departed from the temple: and his disciples came to him for to shew him the buildings of the temple.<br><br>2- And Jesus said unto them, See ye not all these things? verily I say unto you, There shall not be left here one stone upon another, that shall not be thrown down. | 1 And as he went out of the temple, one of his disciples saith unto him, Master, see what manner of stones and what buildings are here!<br><br>2 And Jesus answering said unto him, Seest thou these great buildings? there shall not be left one stone upon another, that shall not be thrown down. | 5 And as some spake of the temple, how it was adorned with goodly stones and gifts, he said,<br><br>6 As for these things which ye behold, the days will come, in the which there shall not be left one stone upon another, that shall not be thrown down. |
| 3 And as he sat upon the mount of Olives, the disciples came unto him privately, saying, Tell us, when shall these things be? and what shall be the sign of thy coming, and of the end of the world? | 3 And as he sat upon the mount of Olives over against the temple, Peter and James and John and Andrew asked him privately,<br><br>4 Tell us, when shall these things be? and what shall be the sign when all these things shall be fulfilled? | 7 And they asked him, saying, Master, but when shall these things be? and what sign will there be when these things shall come to pass? |
| 4 And Jesus answered and said unto them, Take heed that no man deceive you.<br><br>5 For many shall come in my name, saying, I am Christ; and shall deceive many. | 5 And Jesus answering them began to say, Take heed lest any man deceive you:<br><br>6 For many shall come in my name, saying, I am Christ; and shall deceive many. | 8 And he said, Take heed that ye be not deceived: for many shall come in my name, saying, I am Christ; and the time draweth near: go ye not therefore after them. |

| | | |
|---|---|---|
| 6 And ye shall hear of wars and rumours of wars: see that ye be not troubled: for all these things must come to pass, but the end is not yet. | 7 And when ye shall hear of wars and rumours of wars, be ye not troubled: for such things must needs be; but the end shall not be yet. | 9 But when ye shall hear of wars and commotions, be not terrified: for these things must first come to pass; but the end is not by and by. |
| 7 For nation shall rise against nation, and kingdom against kingdom: and there shall be famines, and pestilences, and earthquakes, in divers places.<br><br>8 All these are the beginning of sorrows. | 8 For nation shall rise against nation, and kingdom against kingdom: and there shall be earthquakes in divers places, and there shall be famines and troubles: these are the beginnings of sorrows. | 10 Then said he unto them, Nation shall rise against nation, and kingdom against kingdom:<br><br>11 And great earthquakes shall be in divers places, and famines, and pestilences; and fearful sights and great signs shall there be from heaven. |
| 9 Then shall they deliver you up to be afflicted, and shall kill you: and ye shall be hated of all nations for my name's sake.<br><br>10And then shall many be offended, and shall betray one another, and shall hate one another. | 9 But take heed to yourselves: for they shall deliver you up to councils; and in the synagogues ye shall be beaten: and ye shall be brought before rulers and kings for my sake, for a testimony against them. | 12 But before all these, they shall lay their hands on you, and persecute you, delivering you up to the synagogues, and into prisons, being brought before kings and rulers for my name's sake.<br><br>13 And it shall turn to you for a testimony. |

| | | |
|---|---|---|
| 14 And this gospel of the kingdom shall be preached in all the world for a witness unto all nations; and then shall the end come. | 10 And the gospel must first be published among all nations. | |
| 11 And many false prophets shall rise, and shall deceive many.<br><br>12 And because iniquity shall abound, the love of many shall wax cold.<br><br>13 But he that shall endure unto the end, the same shall be saved. | 21 And then if any man shall say to you, Lo, here is Christ; or, lo, he is there; believe him not:<br><br>22 For false Christs and false prophets shall rise, and shall shew signs and wonders, to seduce, if it were possible, even the elect.<br><br>23 But take ye heed: behold, I have foretold you all things. | |
| | 11 But when they shall lead you, and deliver you up, take no thought beforehand what ye shall speak, neither do ye premeditate: but whatsoever shall be given you in that hour, that speak ye: for it is not ye that speak, but the Holy Ghost. | 14 Settle it therefore in your hearts, not to meditate before what ye shall answer:<br><br>15 For I will give you a mouth and wisdom, which all your adversaries shall not be able to gainsay nor resist. |

| | | |
|---|---|---|
| | 12 Now the brother shall betray the brother to death, and the father the son; and children shall rise up against their parents, and shall cause them to be put to death. | 16 And ye shall be betrayed both by parents, and brethren, and kinsfolks, and friends; and some of you shall they cause to be put to death. |
| | 13 And ye shall be hated of all men for my name's sake: but he that shall endure unto the end, the same shall be saved. | 17 And ye shall be hated of all men for my name's sake.<br><br>18 But there shall not an hair of your head perish.<br><br>19 In your patience possess ye your souls. |
| | | 20 And when ye shall see Jerusalem compassed with armies, then know that the desolation thereof is nigh. |
| 15 When ye therefore shall see the abomination of desolation, spoken of by Daniel the prophet, stand in the holy place, (whoso readeth, let him understand:)<br><br>16 Then let them which be in Judaea flee into the mountains:<br><br>17 Let him which is on the housetop not come down to take any thing out of his house: | 14 But when ye shall see the abomination of desolation, spoken of by Daniel the prophet, standing where it ought not, (let him that readeth understand,) then let them that be in Judaea flee to the mountains:<br><br>15 And let him that is on the housetop not go down into the house, neither enter therein, to take any thing out of his house: | |

18 Neither let him which is in the field return back to take his clothes.

19 And woe unto them that are with child, and to them that give suck in those days!

20 But pray ye that your flight be not in the winter, neither on the sabbath day:

21 For then shall be great tribulation, such as was not since the beginning of the world to this time, no, nor ever shall be.

22 And except those days should be shortened, there should no flesh be saved: but for the elect's sake those days shall be shortened.

23 Then if any man shall say unto you, Lo, here is Christ, or there; believe it not.

16 And let him that is in the field not turn back again for to take up his garment.

17 But woe to them that are with child, and to them that give suck in those days!

18 And pray ye that your flight be not in the winter.

19 For in those days shall be affliction, such as was not from the beginning of the creation which God created unto this time, neither shall be.

20 And except that the Lord had shortened those days, no flesh should be saved: but for the elect's sake, whom he hath chosen, he hath shortened the days.

| | | |
|---|---|---|
| 24 For there shall arise false Christs, and false prophets, and shall shew great signs and wonders; insomuch that, if it were possible, they shall deceive the very elect.<br><br>25 Behold, I have told you before.<br><br>26 Wherefore if they shall say unto you, Behold, he is in the desert; go not forth: behold, he is in the secret chambers; believe it not. | | |
| 29 Immediately after the tribulation of those days shall the sun be darkened, and the moon shall not give her light, and the stars shall fall from heaven, and the powers of the heavens shall be shaken: | 24 But in those days, after that tribulation, the sun shall be darkened, and the moon shall not give her light,<br><br>25 And the stars of heaven shall fall, and the powers that are in heaven shall be shaken. | 25 And there shall be signs in the sun, and in the moon, and in the stars; and upon the earth distress of nations, with perplexity; the sea and the waves roaring;<br><br>26 Men's hearts failing them for fear, and for looking after those things which are coming on the earth: for the powers of heaven shall be shaken. |

| | | |
|---|---|---|
| 27 For as the lightning cometh out of the east, and shineth even unto the west; so shall also the coming of the Son of man be.<br><br>28 For wheresoever the carcase is, there will the eagles be gathered together.<br><br>30 And then shall appear the sign of the Son of man in heaven: and then shall all the tribes of the earth mourn, and they shall see the Son of man coming in the clouds of heaven with power and great glory.<br><br>31 And he shall send his angels with a great sound of a trumpet, and they shall gather together his elect from the four winds, from one end of heaven to the other. | 26 And then shall they see the Son of man coming in the clouds with great power and glory.<br><br>27 And then shall he send his angels, and shall gather together his elect from the four winds, from the uttermost part of the earth to the uttermost part of heaven. | 27 And then shall they see the Son of man coming in a cloud with power and great glory.<br><br>28 And when these things begin to come to pass, then look up, and lift up your heads; for your redemption draweth nigh. |

| | | |
|---|---|---|
| 34 Verily I say unto you, This generation shall not pass, till all these things be fulfilled.<br><br>35 Heaven and earth shall pass away, but my words shall not pass away. | 30 Verily I say unto you, that this generation shall not pass, till all these things be done.<br><br>31 Heaven and earth shall pass away: but my words shall not pass away. | 32 Verily I say unto you, This generation shall not pass away, till all be fulfilled.<br><br>33 Heaven and earth shall pass away: but my words shall not pass away. |
| 36 But of that day and hour knoweth no man, no, not the angels of heaven, but my Father only.<br><br>37 But as the days of Noe were, so shall also the coming of the Son of man be. | 32 But of that day and that hour knoweth no man, no, not the angels which are in heaven, neither the Son, but the Father.<br><br>33 Take ye heed, watch and pray: for ye know not when the time is. | |

# APPENDIX 10

# THE 1ST AND 2ND RESURRECTIONS

The 1ˢᵗ resurrection. Rev 20:4-6.

> 4 And I saw thrones, and they sat upon them, and judgment was given unto them: and **I saw the souls of them that were beheaded for the witness of Jesus, and for the word of God, and which had not worshipped the beast, neither his image, neither had received his mark upon their foreheads, or in their hands; and they lived and reigned with Christ a thousand years.**

> 5 But **the rest of the dead lived not again until the thousand years were finished. This is the first resurrection.**

> 6 Blessed and holy is he that hath part in the first resurrection: on such the second death hath no power, but they shall be priests of God and of Christ, and **shall reign with him a thousand years.**

The good guys reigned with Jesus 1,000 years. They were,

1 - Those resurrected when Jesus died. Matt 27:52-53.

2 – Jesus.

3 – Those raptured.

4 – Those Jesus led out of Sheol. Eph 4:8-11.

5 – and those that were resurrected and appeared to many.

Christians will be part of the heavenly priesthood and have duties. Eph 4:10-11.

> 10 He that descended is the same also that ascended up far above all heavens, that he might fill all things.).
>
> 11 And **he gave some, apostles; and some, prophets; and some, evangelists; and some, pastors and teachers;**

Some people think of heaven as a place where they lounge around all day listening to harps and smelling the roses. Jesus assigned them to five different jobs.

Those that were raptured and those that made it through the Great Tribulation will reign with Jesus during the 1,000 years. They have no concern with the 2$^{nd}$ resurrection. The first resurrection began with Jesus. The 2$^{nd}$ resurrection. Rev 20:12-15.

> 12 And I saw the dead, small and great, stand before God; and **the books were opened:** and **another book was opened, which is the book of life:** and

the **dead were judged out of those things which were written in the books, according to their works.**

13 And the sea gave up the dead which were in it; and death and hell delivered up the dead which were in them: and they were judged every man according to their works.

14 And death and hell were cast into the lake of fire. **This is the second death.**

15 And **whosoever was not found written in the book of life was cast into the lake of fire.**

Let's graph what was said.

**God's Books** (Evaluates works) God's **Book** of Life (Either you are saved or not.)

Suppose you are a Christian because you accepted Jesus as your savior by faith and not works i.e., there was nothing you could do to earn it. Eph 2:8-9. The question now is what kind of a Christian were you? We may ask,

> If I was on trial for being a Christian, would there be enough evidence to convict me?

Sometimes you can't tell the difference between a Christian and a non-Christian. A Christian is one that lives the Christian life to the best of his/her ability. You are not a soldier if all you do is take the oath of allegiance but not salute the flag, obey orders or wear the uniform. True Christians don't rely on faith alone. James 2:14,-17.

14 What *doth it* profit, my brethren, though a man say he hath faith, and have not works? can faith save him?

15 If a brother or sister be naked, and destitute of daily food,

16 And one of you say unto them, Depart in peace, be ye warmed and filled; notwithstanding ye give them not those things which are needful to the body; what doth it profit?

**17 Even so faith, if it hath not works, is dead, being alone.**

Faith is,

Forsake

All

I

Trust

Him

Faith and works are like blades on a pair of scissors. Both are necessary. Faith is something Christians do. It is a verb.

# APPENDIX 11

# RECORDED DEATHS
# IN REVELATION

| VERSE | ACTIVITY | DEATHS |
|---|---|---|
| Rev 6:7-8 | The horse rider was given permission to kil ¼ of all people. | ¼ X 8B = 2B. 6B survive. |
| Rev 9:3-19 | Four demonic angels have permission to kill 1/3 of all people. | 1/3 X 6B = 2B. 4B survive. |
| Rev 810-11 | 84,000 die in 3 days due to bad water. | 4,000,916,000 survive |
| Rev 11:11-13 | 7,000 killed when two witnesses ascend. | 4,000,909,000 survive Can yo find more> |

| NOTES | 3,416,491,667 is nearly ½ of 7.5B which, is what we started with. In order to bring this to reality, we will take ½ of the USA population or ½ X 330M = 165,000,000 die. There were many more deaths that were not recorded. Rev. 16:19. |
| --- | --- |

19And the great city was divided into three parts, and the cities of the nations fell: and great Babylon came in remembrance before God, to give unto her the cup of the wine of the fierceness of his wrath.

The United Nations has 195 member nations. Some are large with many large cities while others are quite small. If we allow two cities per nation, that would equate to nearly 400 cities.

Some of the larger cities are Tokyo, Japan (37M), Delhi, India (29M), Shanghi, China (26M), Sao Paulo, Brazil (22M) totaling 114M. Some of the larger countries are the USA (360M) and China (1.4B) totaling 1.76B.

It is obvious that millions or billions will die. God's vengeance will certainly be aimed at communist nations. Russia has stated that Communism and religion cannot dwell together and that one of them must die.

# APPENDIX 12

# QUICK REFERENCE, INFORMATION AND NOTES

| VERSE | MEANING | VERSE | MEANING | VERSE | MEANING |
|-------|---------|-------|---------|-------|---------|
| 1:5 | Christ is the prince of the kings of the earth | 1:18 | Christ has the keys to heaven and hell. | 1:20 | The 7 stars are the angels/pastors of the 7 churches. The 7 candlesticks are the 7 churches. |
| 2:10 | Crown of Life given to martyrs. | 3.5 | He that overcomes shall wear white | 3:10 | The church at Philadelphia is exempted from the tribulation. |

| | | | | | |
|---|---|---|---|---|---|
| 3:12 | The New Jerusalem that descends from heaven – home of the Christians. | 4.2 | God appeared to John as the colors jasper, sardine stone with a green rainbow. | 4.3 | He that sat on the throne looked like jasper sardine with a green rainbow. |
| 4-4 | 24 elders = 12 apostles + 12 heads of 12 tribes. | 4.5 | 7 lamps = the 7 spirits of God. | 4:6-9 | 4 beast = lion (fierce), calf (strength, man (intelligence), eagle (swiftness) |
| 5:5 | Jesus is the root of David and the lion of the tribe of Judah. | 5.6 | Jesus eyes are the 7 spirits of God. The trinity. | 5:8 | Golden vials full of odors = prayers of the saints. |
| 5:10 | Christians reign as high priests with Christ on earth during the Jewish here-after. | 6:2-8 | The four horses See note 23 | 7.4 | 144,000 Jewish evangelists sealed |

| 7:13-17 See note 7 | The 144,000 escape the tribulation unharmed. | 9:1-11 | Locust came out of the bottom to torture men 5 months. The king of the pit was;Abaddo (Hebrew0, Apollyon (Greek) | 11:3-14 | The two witnesses |
|---|---|---|---|---|---|
| 12;1-6 | The pregnant woman (Israel) with child (Jesus) and the Red Dragon (Satan) | 12:7-9 | Red Dragon = Satan, Loses a war with Michel. | 13:1 | Antichrist emerges from the sea. |
| 13:5-8 | Antichrist attacks God and the people worship Antichrist. | 13:11-18 | False prophet emerges from the earth People wear the 666 mark | 14:1-5 14:14-19 | 144,000 Wheat and grape harvest |

| | | | | | | | |
|---|---|---|---|---|---|---|---|
| 16:12 | The 6th angel pours out his bowl. The Euphrates dries up allowing kings of the east to cross. | 16:13-16 See note21 | The evil trinity (dragon, beast and false prophet) had frogs coming out of their mouths which are the spirits of devils to draw kings of the world to fight Israel at Amrageddon. See note #5 | 17:3-18 | | The Harlot is Babylon. See note 15 and 2' | |
| 18:1-3 | When the tribulation ends, the anti-christ destroys the harlot | 19:7-10 | The marriage of Jesus to the church is announced. | 19:20 | | The beast (antichrist) and the False prpophet are thrown into the Lake of Fire. | |
| 20:1-3 | Satan is bund for 1,000 years. | 20:4 | Martyred saints reigne with Christ 1000 years | 20:7-9 | | Satan released. The Gog/Magog war | |
| 20:1-15 | The Great White Throne judgement. | 21:1 | New earth, New heaven. No sea. | 21:16-27 | | New Jerusalem and heaven described. | |

**THE END**

Printed in the United States
by Baker & Taylor Publisher Services